Disney EATS

Lilo's Tropical Fruit Cones with Kahlúa Drizzle (page 66)

Disney EATS

MORE THAN **150 RECIPES** FOR EVERYDAY **COOKING** AND **INSPIRED FUN**

JOY HOWARD

INTRODUCTION BY **JOY WILSON,** AKA **JOY THE BAKER**

Disney EDITIONS

Los Angeles · New York

PHOTOGRAPHY: Joanna Chattman   **FOOD STYLING:** Joy Howard

PROP STYLING: Ann Lewis   **PHOTO ASSISTANT:** Georgia Teensma, Montgomery Sheridan

FOOD STYLING ASSISTANTS: Laura Manning, Kaitlyn Ferrari

RECIPES BY: Joy Howard; Disney Family editors; the chefs at Be Our Guest, The Crystal Palace, and Disney's Polynesian Village Resort; Meredith Bond Steele; Shelby Chambers; Tiffany Davis; Rosie DeLibero; Li Ming Lee; Vickie Liu; Jessica McDonald; Kate O'Leary; Irene Lee; Jen Wood; and Elise Apffel

COVER DESIGN: David Roe

INTERIOR DESIGN: Laura Palese, David Roe

ISBN 978-1-368-04919-1
FAC-029191-20192
First Hardcover Edition, October 2020
Printed in Malaysia
10 9 8 7 6 5 4 3 2 1

Visit www.disneybooks.com

SUSTAINABLE FORESTRY INITIATIVE

Certified Chain of Custody
At Least 20% Certified Forest Content
www.sfiprogram.org
SFI-00993
For Text Only

For **CHRIS**, the **GIRLS**, and every person who chooses to cook (and live) with imagination.

Pop Stars (page 64)

M and M Milk
Toppers
(page 239)

Woody's
Cowboy Chili
(page 127)

CONTENTS

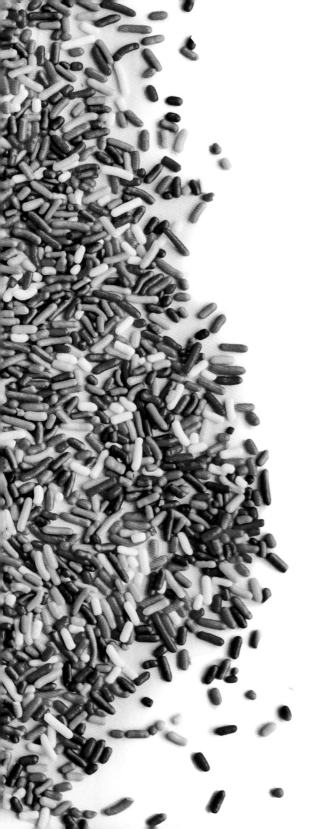

INTRODUCTION BY
Joy Wilson,
aka Joy the Baker

I grew up in Los Angeles, exactly 32.6 miles from Disneyland—a short jaunt from the happiest place on earth. I know the exact mileage, because when I was ten I distinctly remember negotiating whether or not that journey could be done on my little pink and lavender bike. I had just taken off the training wheels, so surely I was ready for this *Homeward Bound*-style trek.

I never did make *that* journey on my bike, but my family and I were lucky enough to go to Disneyland, with great fanfare . . . twice a year! My parents made sure to let us know what a treat it was to visit with Mickey and Minnie for an entire day, as I'm sure it was something they saved for with each month of work. My sister and I would wake up early and put on our favorite Disney movie. I'd always vote for *Beauty and the Beast*; my sister, who likely wanted to watch *The Lion King* for the umpteenth time, would ultimately cede to me—her bossy elder. We'd waltz around the house singing the opening song from *Beauty* while my parents lovingly packed sandwiches for all of us in the kitchen.

We'd be buzzing with excitement on the way to the park. Our tradition heading there was to stop at the grocery store, where my sister and I were allowed to buy one drink and one bag of chips each (to go with our special Disneyland-day sandwiches). It might seem like a small treat now, but my parents were early health food adopters, so a soda and chips were a big deal in our young lives.

We'd spend the morning at the park, likely seeing how many times we could go on the Matterhorn, before we'd sneak back to the family Jeep to take a rest and eat our sandwiches, gulp down our "special" drinks, and munch on our chips. Mom had written our favorite characters' names on each sandwich wrapper. So, even though we weren't eating cheeseburgers in the park, our family tradition felt so special. Why? Our Disney experience wasn't just inside the park—it also involved eating homemade sandwiches while dangling our legs off the back end of a Jeep . . . in the park's then expansive parking lot.

Once back in the park after lunch, we all knew we were heading—without hesitation—to New Orleans Square for Mickey beignets. They were the absolute highlight of my time at Disneyland . . . and maybe why I live in New Orleans today.

Our time at Disneyland was incredibly special to our family. My parents made a day trip to the park an entire family extravaganza, complete with homemade sandwiches and a big dinner we all would make together after we got home—tired yet exhilarated.

It's funny how memories take shape, how the small act of my mom writing *Belle* on the paper towel that held my homemade sandwich solidifies in my memory with such love.

10

The joy of Disney is that it can take us to another world, altogether. I was certain I was in another world at New Orleans Square eating beignets with my family, just as I was able to escape, albeit briefly, to another place while watching *The Little Mermaid* at home in my living room. (Can you tell that I'm an old-school Disney lover?)

Well, those simple but transcendent moments can also be created in the kitchen, with these easy Disney-inspired recipes. Playful, energized cooking doesn't have to be reserved for fancy weekend breakfasts or Sunday suppers. There is real joy that can come from the kitchen on a seemingly mundane Tuesday, too! The recipes within this book are meant to be simple and adaptable to whatever you might have tucked away in your pantry or vegetable drawer. From Mickey's Taco Cones and Mamá Coco's Empanadas to Captain Hook Brownie Bites and Under the Sea Lollipops, you'll find everyday recipes everyone in the family can enjoy. Every recipe is meant to inspire that spark of Disney magic and celebrate togetherness, even on the most routine of days.

Chefs hold all sorts of secret ingredients on their shelves to make their dishes pop. This book (and a pair of Mickey ears to wear perhaps while in the kitchen preparing things) is your secret ingredient and sprinkle of magic. You can unlock a world of Disney magic creating joy and a trove of memories from your very own kitchen, every single day—even if it's just a simple sandwich that you devour in the back seat of the car.

You'll discover there's Disney sparkle to be found everywhere.

A NOTE FROM
THE AUTHOR

The Mad Hatter's TWISTED TEA PARTY; the spaghetti scene from *Lady and the Tramp*; the ANIMATED FEAST OF FRENCH DELIGHTS in *Beauty and the Beast*. Food has played a central role in SHAPING THE STORIES of some of Disney's most beloved characters, and at times has even helped define their PERSONALITIES. Who would POOH be without his constant hankering for HONEY? What would inspire Remy without his dream of becoming a GREAT CHEF?

It's fitting, then, that we've come up with a collection of recipes celebrating the characters of the Disney universe. The recipes in this book are meant to bring more joy and wonder to the way you eat—whether that means garnishing a bowl of hot cereal with a strawberry flower (see page 35) or pairing the next Friday-night viewing of your favorite Disney film with a character-inspired snack (see page 64).

We've developed and tested (and tested some more!) recipes to create ideas that aren't just for special occasions, but also your weekday repertoire. Our book is organized by meal to help you easily find what you need—from quick-fix breakfasts to birthday-worthy treats. While our recipes do feature a handful of ambitious projects (check out the lofty cake inspired by

Sleeping Beauty on page 266!), we know that most home cooks want recipes that are easy to make and include simple-to-find ingredients, and that even though there's no harm in the occasional indulgence, wholesome food matters. This collection reflects that.

Cooking requires creativity, so don't be afraid to use your own. Think of this book not just as an instruction manual for learning something new, but also as an invitation for using what you already know. Make ingredient substitutions if you like, cut corners if you need to, or add a little touch of something that will make a recipe all your own. Like the stories and characters that belong to the Disney family, we want the food you find here to inspire you, and we hope it encourages more happiness in your kitchen and around the table.

13

THE PLAYBOOK

YOU DON'T NEED A CULINARY DEGREE to be a success in the kitchen or become a master at making any of the recipes in this book. But we've compiled some TIPS AND TRICKS to help ensure you get the RESULTS YOU WANT—including clever hacks that will help you decorate sweets like a pro.

GENERAL TIPS

- **Read through the whole recipe.** Discovering that you're missing an ingredient in the middle of making a dish can take the fun right out of cooking, not to mention add lots of extra time or even ruin a recipe. Be sure to review all the ingredients and read through all the steps before you cook so you can make sure you have everything you need on hand.

- **Don't rush.** Cooking good food can't be done in a hurry and much of the joy can be found in the process.

- **Take shortcuts if you need to.** Shortcuts can be a real game changer in getting the results you want in the time that you have. Making a whole batch of cute cupcakes from scratch is fun but can also be an ambitious project. Using boxed cake mix or canned frosting can yield results that look just as sweet as anything you make from scratch, so feel free to use them.

- **Be cautious when cooking with kids.** Most recipes in this book include prep and cooking steps that are appropriate to do with kids, but sharp knives and working with heat require more skilled (read: mature) hands. Cook alongside the little ones in your life. It's fun and time well spent!

- **Improvise!** With the exception of baking, most recipes aren't written in a way that discourages improvisation. Feel empowered to make ingredient swaps, use what you like or what you have on hand, or omit ingredients as you wish. Recipes for baked goods should not be altered, though; they rely heavily on precise ingredient ratios.

14

THREE ESSENTIAL TIPS FOR EMBELLISHING SAVORY FOOD

- **Keep things covered.** Sliced fruits and veggies have a tendency to dry out as they sit. Keep them covered with a damp paper towel as you work so they stay looking fresh.

- **Substitutions are okay.** But keep it sensible. Ingredient combinations should be as appetizing as they are appealing to the eye.

- **Use this trick for perfect portions:** If working with items like dough that must be evenly divided, start by halving it, then evenly split each portion once again, and so on to yield consistently sized results.

EVEN MORE TIPS FOR DECORATING CAKES AND OTHER SWEETS

- **Take the time for a crumb coat.** A crumb coat—lightly frosting the cake and then chilling it briefly so that the icing sets—will help you get a smoother final coat for your cake. Don't skip this step!

- **Warm candies for easier rolling.** Chewy candies aren't always soft when you buy them. If you need to roll out pieces for decorating, they can be microwaved in 5-second bursts (don't go longer—they will melt!) to make them pliable. Dust your work surface with a sprinkle of powdered sugar if they get sticky.

- **One treat at a time.** In nearly every cupcake recipe, we emphasize decorating one at a time from start to finish. This is because icing has a tendency to become less tacky as it sits. It may be slightly less efficient, but trust us when we say this is the best (and least frustrating) approach for embellishing sweets.

- **Keep it chill.** Once dough is shaped, whether for cookies or a piecrust, pop it in the freezer for 10 minutes. This will help prevent extra spreading or slumping from happening as the dough bakes.

- **There's a big difference between white and vanilla.** In the case of both boxed cake and frosting, the latter tends to have a yellowish hue. If you're using store-bought products for your treats and you plan to color them, be sure to opt for white so it doesn't throw off the food dye.

- **Speaking of frosting . . .** If you're doing it by hand, put the frosting in the fridge for 20 minutes to firm up slightly. It will be easier to work with and smooth over.

- **And about that food dye . . .** The most important things you should know are the following: Natural dyes are beautiful, but the colors tend to be more muted than the manufactured stuff. Gel dyes are by far the best for achieving saturated color with the least amount of dye. They also come in a larger variety of hues. Liquid dye is perfectly acceptable; you'll just need a lot more of it.

WORKING WITH CHOCOLATE

- **Keep water away.** Water is the enemy of melted chocolate. Make sure you're working with dry equipment or you'll end up with a seized and crumbly mess.

- **Be careful with the temperature.** Chocolate begins to soften around 86°F and is very sensitive to extreme heat. If you're melting it on the stove top, use a double boiler (you can make one yourself by fitting a bowl over a pot of simmering water) so that it doesn't scorch. If you're melting it in the microwave, warm it in short bursts and stir, stir, stir in between each heating to melt it completely.

- **Splurge on the good stuff.** Higher quality chocolate melts better and maintains a more consistent viscosity as it cools. You don't have to buy the most expensive stuff you can find, but we've discovered that opting for finer chocolate is money well spent.

- **A little oil goes a long way.** If needed, you can add a drop or two to melted chocolate (but no more!) to make it more viscous for drizzling.

HELPFUL TOOLS

NEARLY ALL THE RECIPES in this book can be accomplished with basic kitchen equipment, but sometimes a simple tool can be a REAL GAME CHANGER. We've compiled a list of some SUPER-HELPFUL but not-at-all-fancy items that are worth seeking out.

- **Bamboo skewers**
  Available in a variety of sizes, skewers aren't just for impaling fruit and veggies. Use them as a tool for making (or starting) holes in ingredients when you're decorating or for moving around teensy items like sprinkles. They're also perfect for holding stacked items in place so they don't topple over.

- **Cake turntable**
  It's true that this item really only has one use, but if you're inspired to take up cake decorating as a hobby it's well worth having. The stand is the best (and really only) way to ensure an extra smooth surface around the sides and top of a cake.

- **Food molds**
  Thanks to the explosion of interest in cake and sweets decorating, you can find food molds in nearly any shape or size. Use them for chocolate, fondant, baked treats, or even fancy ice cubes.

- **Kitchen shears**
  A good pair of scissors made exclusively for the kitchen are a super-versatile tool. Aside from snipping herbs or candies, they can make quick work of tasks like cutting pizza or trimming long noodles into bite-size pieces.

- **Lollipop sticks**
  Keep these on hand for turning smalls sweets into fun-to-eat treats. They're often available in a variety of lengths at craft stores in the cake decorating section. Use them in place of bamboo skewers for younger eaters—no sharp points!

- **Mandolin**
  This extra-sharp tool requires careful handling, but if you're a perfectionist you'll appreciate its precision. It can cut veggies into thin, uniform slices or shred cabbage for slaw.

17

- **Melon baller**

  As the name suggests, the primary use for this tool is shaping fruit. But, we also love to use them to scrape seeds and pulp from manner of veggies—from butternut squash to tomatoes and bell peppers.

- **Mini fondant (or cookie) cutters**

  A set of geometric shapes is well worth keeping on hand for shaping everything—cheese slices, veggies, pita chips, and more.

- **Mini offset spatula**

  This is essential for achieving a camera-worthy, smooth layer of frosting on a cupcake. We also use them for smoothing cake batter in the pan before baking and putting finishing touches on piped chocolate or royal icing.

- **Mini rolling pin**

  A standard size rolling pin is handy, but for flattening chewy candies or smaller items we like to use a mini pin. It offers more agility and the ends can also double as a tamper for pressing dough into cupcake wells.

- **Parchment paper**

  If you bake, you're likely familiar with the benefit of using parchment as a nonstick surface in cake pans or on baking sheets. You can also use it for piping chocolate shapes (they peel off perfectly once set) and measuring messy dry ingredients like flour. For the latter, place a sheet down on your work surface to catch spills, then use the paper to funnel the ingredient back into its container.

- **Paring knife**

  You don't need a fancy one, but choosing a nice knife with an extra sharp tip will make shaping fruits and veggies much easier.

- **Pastry brush**
  Silicone brushes offer simpler cleanup, but natural bristles yield the most even results; take your pick! Aside from brushing washes on baked goods, you can use these to sweep away crumbs from a serving platter before you set it out.

- **Piping bags and tips**
  If you're not too particular, you can use a plastic bag with the corner snipped off for creating dots and lines. For the most professional-looking results, however, you'll want to use a piping bag fit with a writing tip. Fancier tips shaped like a star or grass will help you take your treats to the next level.

- **Scoops**
  With a few different sizes on hand, you can portion everything from meatballs to cookie dough and cake batter. Look for ones with a release to make the job hands-free.

- **Standard and mini muffin tins**
  Using these to bake cupcakes is a no-brainer, but did you know they also make great catchalls when you're doing lots of decorating? Place sprinkles, sugars, and other tiny toppings in the wells to keep things tidy while you work.

- **Toothpicks**
  Move around small ingredients, paint super-thin lines of chocolate, or apply small amounts of frosting to a decoration before adhering it to a treat. Toothpicks are a simple tool with a lot of versatility, and we always keep them around.

- **Tweezers**
  Save yourself the frustration of trying to place small, fussy ingredients with your bare hands and invest in a food-safe pair of tweezers. It will make the process not only easier, but much more enjoyable.

- **Veggie peeler**
  This simple prep tool can also be used to cut thin ribbons of fruit or veggies for salad or drink garnishes.

Chapter

1

BREAKFAST and BRUNCH

IT'S THE MOST IMPORTANT MEAL OF THE DAY, so why not break out of the morning doldrums and sprinkle a little fun onto your plate? We know you don't have time for anything too elaborate—it's early, after all!—but adding a dash of whimsy to a feast with friends (see Worry-Free Frittata, page 26) or a meal for one (see Fit for a Princess Smoothie Bowls, page 28) can go a long way in making sure you get off to a great start.

Alien TOAST for TWO

PREP
10 min

COOK
10 min

SERVES
2

Our take on avocado toast is sure to prompt an "ooooooooooh" from any TOY STORY FAN. Pair it with sliced fruit for a satisfying meal.

INGREDIENTS

½ small avocado

Kosher salt

Black pepper

2 slices whole wheat bread

1 tablespoon cream cheese

6 black olives

6 baby spinach leaves

DIRECTIONS

1 In a small bowl, use a fork to mash the avocado until smooth with a few small bits. Season with salt and pepper and stir well. Set aside.

2 Toast the bread slices. Place each slice on a plate, then spoon and spread half the avocado onto each piece as shown.

3 Divide the cream cheese into six portions. Roll each into a ball, flatten it slightly, and arrange three dots on each slice of toast for the eyes. Trim the hatched end from each olive and press one on each dot of cream cheese.

4 Use kitchen shears to trim four of the spinach leaves into ears, and tuck two in place on each slice of toast beneath the avocado. Trim an antenna and mouth from each of the remaining leaves and arrange as shown. Serve immediately.

Helpful TIP

Keep the avocado from browning before you eat by adding a squeeze of lemon or lime juice. The citric acid in the juice helps slow down the oxidation process that causes discoloration.

Bacon & Egg MOUSE-WICH

PREP
10 min

COOK
30 min

SERVES
4

What's better than a **GRAB-AND-GO** breakfast sandwich from a fast-food joint? One you make at home that begins with a **FROM-SCRATCH** biscuit! We've topped this version with the usual fixings but added a handful of **SPINACH** to each sandwich for a boost of green goodness.

INGREDIENTS

6 slices bacon

2 cups flour

4 teaspoons baking powder

1 teaspoon kosher salt

½ cup plus 8 teaspoons margarine

1 cup whole milk

8 teaspoons olive oil

4 large eggs

4 slices cheddar

1 cup baby spinach

Special equipment
Mickey Mouse silicone breakfast mold

DIRECTIONS

1 Heat the oven to 400°F and line a baking sheet with foil. Arrange the bacon in a single layer on the sheet and bake until crisp, about 15 minutes. Transfer to a paper towel-lined plate and set aside.

2 In a large bowl, stir together the flour, baking powder, and salt. Use two knives or a pastry cutter to cut in ½ cup margarine. Blend in the milk until combined.

3 In a cast iron skillet over medium-low heat, melt 2 teaspoons margarine. Center the silicone mold in the skillet and fill with batter. Cook the biscuit covered until browned underneath, about 4 minutes. Remove the mold (carefully, as it will be hot), flip the biscuit, and cook covered until brown on the other side, about 4 minutes more. Continue with the remaining batter and margarine. Halve each biscuit lengthwise.

4 Wipe the skillet clean and warm 2 teaspoons olive oil over medium heat. Crack an egg into the skillet and cook until the whites are set and the center is still slightly runny, about 3 minutes. Slide the egg onto a biscuit half and top with a slice of cheese. Repeat with the remaining eggs, biscuits, and cheese. (If you like, the assembled sandwich halves can be kept warm in a 200°F oven while you make the rest of the eggs.)

5 Halve each slice of bacon and add three pieces to each sandwich. Top off each with ¼ cup spinach and the other biscuit half. Serve immediately.

Worry-Free FRITTATA

PREP
15 min

COOK
25 min

SERVES
8

Please your own pride or a group of **HUNGRY** guests with an all-in-one egg dish that will make them want to **ROAR** for more. In addition to an easy prep, frittata also offers **VERSATILITY,** so you can swap what's in the recipe for any veggies you have on hand—just be sure to **COOK** them first.

INGREDIENTS

3 Yukon Gold potatoes, peeled and diced into ½-inch cubes (about 2 cups)

10 eggs

1 teaspoon kosher salt

2 tablespoons unsalted butter

1 tablespoon finely chopped herbs, such as thyme, parsley, chives, or basil, plus more for garnish

1 heaping cup grated cheddar

Fresh salsa, for serving (optional)

DIRECTIONS

1 Fill a large pot with an inch of water and fit it with a steaming basket. Place the potatoes in the basket and steam, covered, until tender, about 10 minutes. Let cool slightly.

2 Heat the broiler to high. In a small bowl, beat together the eggs and salt. In a 9- or 10-inch skillet over medium-low heat, warm the butter until foamy. Stir the herbs, cheese, and potatoes into the eggs, then pour the mixture into the pan. Cover and cook the frittata until set around the edges but still jiggly in the center, about 12 minutes. Transfer the pan to the broiler and cook until the center is set and the frittata is puffed and browned, about 2 minutes. Serve slices hot or at room temperature, topped with salsa if desired.

Helpful TIP

It might be tempting to use the russet potatoes you already have in your pantry, but Yukon Gold potatoes are a must. They'll hold their shape better and add more pleasing flavor to the dish.

Fit for a Princess SMOOTHIE BOWLS

UNLEASH YOUR INNER ARTIST and update your Instagram feed by assembling one of these healthy BREAKFAST bowls—each inspired by a different Disney PRINCESS.

Moana's SUNSHINE BOWL

blend:

¼ cup shredded coconut + 1 frozen banana + ¼ cup frozen cantaloupe + ½ cup Greek yogurt + 2 mandarin oranges

top with:

sliced almonds + shredded coconut + blueberries + mandarin orange slices + green grapes

Ariel's DEEP BLUEBERRY SEA BOWL

blend:
1 frozen banana + **½ cup frozen blueberries**
+ **¼ cup Greek yogurt**
+ **splash of milk**

top with:
sliced kiwi + **star fruit** + **strawberries**

Snow White's BEWITCHING APPLE BOWL

blend:
⅓ cup apple juice + **1 frozen banana**
+ **1 cup frozen mango** + **4 ice cubes**

top with:
sliced strawberries and blueberries
+ **half an apple**

Sulley JAM-FILLED TARTS

PREP
15 min

COOK
1 hr *(includes cooling and decorating time)*

MAKES
6

Cause a **SCREAM** at the breakfast table with individual tarts shaped like James P. Sullivan—professional Scarer and fuzzy, **WIDE-EYED** resident of Monstropolis. Serve them at room temperature or beware: warming them up could make the icing melt into a **FRIGHTENING** mess!

INGREDIENTS

1 (15-ounce) package refrigerated piecrust

Flour, for dusting

¼ cup of your favorite fruit preserve

1 large egg

1 batch royal icing (see recipe page 199)

Light blue food coloring

Dark blue food coloring

12 blue candy bananas

DIRECTIONS

1 Heat the oven to 400°F and line a baking sheet with parchment paper. On a lightly floured surface, roll out a piecrust to an even ¼-inch thickness. Use an oval cutter to shape it into 6 ovals and arrange them 2 inches apart on the baking sheet. Gather and reroll the dough as needed.

2 Spoon 2 teaspoons fruit preserve onto the center of each crust. Roll out the remaining crust and shape it with the oval cutter as described in step 1.

3 In a small bowl, whisk together the egg and 1 tablespoon cool water. Brush the edges of each pie on the prepared pan with egg wash, then top with a dough oval and press gently to seal. Use the tines of a fork to crimp the edges of each pie, as shown.

4 Bake the pies until light golden, about 10 minutes. Transfer to a rack and let cool completely. Evenly divide the icing among three small bowls. Tint one light blue and another dark blue. Place each portion of icing, including the remaining white portion, in a piping bag fit with a small writing tip.

5 Working with one pie at a time, cover each with light blue icing, then press two horns in place, as shown. Let the icing set for 10 minutes, then use the white and dark blue icing to add the remaining facial details. Let the icing set between layers as needed and for at least 30 minutes before serving.

Rapunzel's BRAIDED BUNS

PREP
30 min

COOK
1 hr (includes cooling and decorating time)

MAKES
10

Edible **FLOWERS** made of almonds and jam and a dough that's **FILLED** with citrusy orange zest make these twisted buns a **FESTIVE SPRING** side. Serve them as a part of a big breakfast spread or alongside a hot cup of tea.

INGREDIENTS

3 cups flour, plus more for dusting

3 tablespoons sugar

3 teaspoons baking powder

1 teaspoon kosher salt

1 cup whole milk

3 tablespoons vegetable oil

2 teaspoons orange zest

2 large eggs

⅓ cup strawberry or raspberry jam

¼ cup sliced almonds

BRAIDING THE DOUGH HOW-TO

DIRECTIONS

1 Heat the oven to 400°F and line a baking sheet with parchment paper. In a large bowl, whisk together the flour, sugar, baking powder, and salt. In another bowl, whisk together the milk, oil, orange zest, and one egg. Add one third of the wet ingredient mixture into the dry ingredients and stir to combine. Repeat twice, stirring until fully combined between each addition.

2 Turn the dough out onto a lightly floured surface and knead until smooth. Divide the dough into 10 equal portions. Working with one portion at a time, divide it into thirds and roll each piece into a 12-inch rope. Pinch the ropes together on one end and braid, as shown. Transfer to the prepared baking sheet. Repeat with the remaining dough.

3 In a small bowl, whisk together the remaining egg and 1 tablespoon water. Brush the braids with egg wash, then bake until golden, about 10 minutes. Transfer to a rack to cool.

4 Place the jam in a ziplock bag and snip a corner. Pipe a dollop of jam onto a braid, then embellish with almond petals, pressing them into the jam, as shown. Repeat, adding two or more almond flowers to each bun. Serve immediately.

Belle's Enchanted QUINOA PORRIDGE

PREP
15 min

COOK
Overnight
chilling

SERVES
2

Just like **OVERNIGHT OATS**, this straight-from-the-fridge breakfast **MAGICALLY** comes together while you sleep. You'll need to **COOK** the quinoa before it soaks, but the end result— **LIGHTLY SWEETENED** with honey and topped with fresh berries—will be well worth the extra effort.

INGREDIENTS

1 cup cooked quinoa

⅔ cup light coconut milk

½ cup unsweetened chopped dried cherries

2 tablespoons unsweetened shredded coconut

2 teaspoons honey

2 large strawberries

1 banana, sliced

½ cup mixed fresh berries

2 tablespoons toasted sliced almonds

DIRECTIONS

1 In a medium bowl, stir together the quinoa, coconut milk, cherries, shredded coconut, and honey. Refrigerate overnight.

2 Place a strawberry on the end of a fork, leaf side down. With a paring knife, carefully cut staggered slits around the perimeter of the berry to form rose petals as shown below. Use the edge of the knife to pull back the petals slightly and give them dimension. Repeat with the other strawberry.

3 Remove the porridge from the refrigerator and add a few tablespoons water if it is too thick. Divide the porridge between two bowls, then garnish each with half the banana slices, fresh berries, and almonds. Top each with a strawberry rose.

STRAWBERRY FLOWER HOW-TO

Cinderella's Dreamy PUMPKIN WAFFLES

PREP
10 min

COOK
25 min

MAKES
6 waffles

TRANSFORMING a tiny pumpkin into a horse-drawn carriage requires a FAIRY GODMOTHER, but making a batch of these warm, homey waffles can be accomplished by anyone with a few SIMPLE pantry ingredients (including pumpkin, of course!). A sprinkle of pepitas before serving adds a PLEASING CRUNCH to each bite.

INGREDIENTS

1 cup all-purpose flour

1 cup whole wheat flour

1¼ teaspoons baking powder

1½ teaspoons cinnamon

½ teaspoon nutmeg

¼ teaspoon kosher salt

⅓ cup brown sugar

2 tablespoons vegetable oil

1¾ cups light coconut milk

1¾ cups pumpkin puree

2 eggs

Cooking spray

6 (½-inch-thick) slices of a Granny Smith apple

2 tablespoons pepitas, for serving

Maple syrup, for serving

DIRECTIONS

1 Heat a waffle iron. In a large bowl, whisk together the flours, baking powder, cinnamon, nutmeg, and salt. Make a well in the center of the mixture and add the brown sugar, oil, coconut milk, pumpkin puree, and eggs. Gradually whisk the flour into the wet ingredients until combined. Do not overmix.

2 Coat the waffle iron with cooking spray, then ladle batter onto the iron. (The amount will vary depending on the size of your iron.) Cook until golden brown.

3 Trim each apple slice into a stem shape. If you like, add detail to each stem by cutting small slits into it as shown.

4 To serve, place a waffle on a plate and garnish with an apple-slice stem. Top with pepitas and serve immediately with maple syrup.

Eeyore PANCAKE STACK

PREP
5 min

COOK
25 min

MAKES
1 serving

Though the most sullen resident of the Hundred-Acre Wood is FAMOUSLY not much of a morning creature, there are few cuter ways to CAPTURE him than in an Eeyore pancake breakfast. Using a SQUEEZE bottle for the batter will make shaping his face and ears far simpler than using a spoon. If you don't have a squeeze bottle on hand, put the batter in a plastic bag, snip a corner, and PIPE AWAY.

INGREDIENTS

1 cup of your favorite pancake batter

Cooking spray

Chocolate sauce, for garnish

Plain Greek yogurt, for garnish

4 blueberries

Special equipment
Food-grade squeeze bottle

DIRECTIONS

1 Place the batter in the squeeze bottle. Warm a nonstick skillet over medium heat. Coat with cooking spray, then use some of the batter to pipe a rounded diamond-shaped ear in the pan. Cook until bubbly and golden on the underside, about 4 minutes. Flip and continue to cook until golden, about 2 minutes more. Transfer to a plate and repeat, cooking another diamond-shaped ear and an oval for Eeyore's face.

2 To assemble, pipe a bit of chocolate sauce near the edge of a plate for Eeyore's hair, as shown. Set the oval pancake in place just below, then layer the ears on top. Use the yogurt and blueberries to add a pair of eyes and a muzzle, as shown. Finish by piping on more chocolate hair, eyebrows, and a line of chocolate stitching down the center of Eeyore's face. Serve immediately.

Mulan's Sweet and Savory BREAKFAST BOWL

PREP
5 min

COOK
10 min

MAKES
1 serving

On Mulan's first day of **TRAINING**, Mushu wakes her with the cacophonous chirp of a cricket and a **PIPING HOT** bowl of porridge adorned with a smiling face. Recreate the scene with your own version of hot cereal topped with **FRESH FRUIT**, yogurt, and bacon.

INGREDIENTS

Half a peach, canned or fresh, peeled

1 cup prepared hot cereal (We used quick-cooking farina cereal.)

3 tablespoons plain Greek yogurt

1 slice cooked bacon

DIRECTIONS

1 Use a mini round cutter to shape two circles from the peach half. Place the cereal in a bowl. Spoon on two yogurt eyes, as shown, then top each with a peach center. Finish with a bacon strip mouth. Serve immediately.

Judy Hopps's Carrot MUFFINS

PREP
10 min

COOK
30 min

MAKES
12

START the workweek by baking a batch of these portable cakes you can pack to satisfy late-morning MUNCHIES or snack on later in the day. Coarse sugar makes their tops IRRESISTIBLY crunchy (and decadent!), but you can skip it and they'll still be plenty SWEET.

INGREDIENTS

1⅓ cups flour

1½ teaspoons baking powder

¾ cup dark brown sugar, packed

1 teaspoon ground cinnamon

¼ teaspoon kosher salt

½ cup whole milk

2 eggs, room temperature

½ cup coconut oil, melted and cooled slightly

2 tablespoons orange juice

1½ teaspoons vanilla extract

1½ cups shredded carrots (about 3 medium)

¾ cup walnuts, chopped

Coarse sugar, for topping (optional)

DIRECTIONS

1 Heat the oven to 375°F and line a muffin tin with paper liners. In a large bowl, whisk together the flour, baking powder, brown sugar, cinnamon, and salt. In another bowl, whisk together the milk, eggs, oil, orange juice, and vanilla. Add the milk mixture to the dry ingredients and stir to combine. Fold in the carrots and walnuts.

2 Evenly divide the batter among the prepared muffin wells. If using coarse sugar, sprinkle it over the batter. Bake until a toothpick inserted in the center of a muffin comes out clean, about 25 minutes. Let cool in the pan 5 minutes, then transfer to a rack to cool completely.

Chapter

2

SIPS and SNACKS

CURB MIDDAY HUNGER OR INDULGE YOUR ANYTIME CRAVINGS WITH FRESH AND FUN TAKES ON SNACKS AND DRINKS,

from quick-fix healthy bites (see Hidden Mickey Apple Slice Sandwiches, page 61) to grown-up, guilt-free cocktails (see Fairy-Tale Sippers, page 50).

King of All VEGGIE PLATTERS

PREP 10 min

COOK 10 min

SERVES 2

Please growling stomachs—and **SIMBA FANS**—with a **REGAL SPREAD** featuring healthy veggies and dip. Strips of bell pepper make **SIMBA'S WAVY MANE**, but if you're not a fan you can achieve a similar look with baby carrots.

INGREDIENTS

1 (8-inch) whole wheat tortilla

1 red radish

¼ cup of your favorite hummus

½ red bell pepper, ribs and seeds removed

2 pitted black olives

Helpful **TIP**

You can't make this ferociously cute platter in advance, but you can get ahead on the prep. Cut the pepper strips for the mane, then wrap them in a wet paper towel and seal in a ziplock bag. The peppers will stay crisp for at least two days.

DIRECTIONS

1 Use a 3-inch round cookie cutter to shape two circles from the tortilla. With kitchen shears, snip one round in half to form Simba's mouth, then trim the other round to form the bridge of Simba's nose, as shown.

2 Cut two 1½-inch rounds from the remaining tortilla for the ears. Halve the radish and slice two thin rounds from one portion for the eyes. Trim the remaining half in the shape of a nose.

3 Spread the hummus in a circle in the center of a plate. Place the tortilla nose and mouth, and radish eyes and nose, as shown. Cut the pepper into curved strips and arrange around the hummus. Add the tortilla ears and finish with sliced olive pupils and olive strip eyebrows.

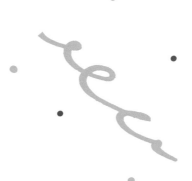

Lady and the Tramp
PUPPY MIX

PREP
5 min

COOK
5 min

SERVES
4

MUCH LIGHTER—AND EASIER TO MAKE!—than a plate of spaghetti and meatballs, this simple mix will satisfy your craving for something CRUNCHY. The recipe EASILY DOUBLES, so you can make a big batch to share with hungry game-night guests.

INGREDIENTS

1 cup whole-grain O-shaped cereal

3 cups popped popcorn

1 cup of your favorite nuts

1 cup mini pretzel twists

DIRECTIONS

Toss together the ingredients in a large bowl and serve.

FAIRY-TALE SIPPERS

Toast to your **FAVORITE** character with an everyone-can-imbibe **MOCKTAIL**. Blended with ingredients like fresh fruit and herbs, each one offers easy drinking for your next **PARTY** or end-of-the-day **ENJOYMENT**.

Spirit-Free
Serengeti Spritz
(page 52)

Mock Mai Tai
(page 52)

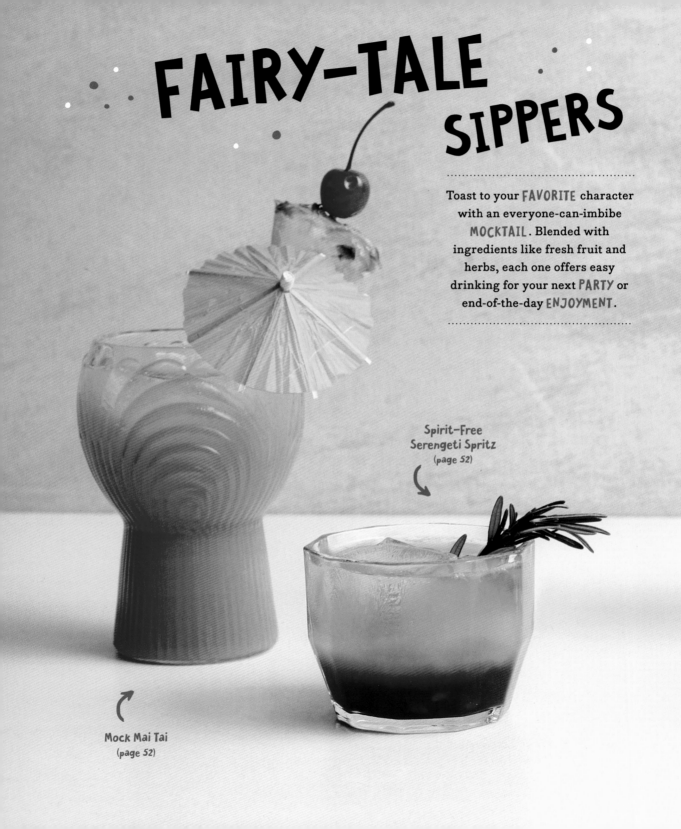

Belle's Booze-less
French 75
(page 52)

Jack-Jack
Strawberry
Milk Punch
(page 53)

Yeti's Yellow Lemon
Slush
(page 53)

Spirit-Free SERENGETI SPRITZ

PREP: 5 min • COOK: 5 min • SERVES: 2

INGREDIENTS

3 sprigs fresh rosemary, broken into pieces, plus more for garnish

6 ounces mango juice

6 ounces fresh-squeezed orange juice

Juice of 1 lime

1¼ ounces simple syrup (See recipe at right)

4 ounces pomegranate juice

2 tablespoons pomegranate seeds

Club soda

DIRECTIONS

1 In a drink shaker, muddle the rosemary, then add the mango, orange, and lime juice, along with the simple syrup and ¼ cup ice. Shake to blend.

2 Fill two rock glasses halfway with ice and add half the pomegranate juice and seeds to each glass. Evenly divide the mango mixture between the two glasses, pouring it in slowly for a layered effect. Top off each drink with club soda. Garnish with a sprig of rosemary, then serve.

Mock MAI TAI

PREP: 5 min • COOK: 5 min • SERVES: 2

INGREDIENTS

10 ounces orange juice

2½ ounces lime juice

½ ounce orgeat syrup

1 ounce grenadine

1 ounce simple syrup (See recipe at right)

½ ounce cream of coconut

Pineapple slice, for garnish

2 maraschino cherries, for garnish

DIRECTIONS

1 In a drink shaker, combine all the ingredients with ¼ cup ice. Shake to blend.

2 Fill two rock glasses halfway with ice and divide the cocktail evenly between the glasses. Garnish each with a segment of the pineapple slice and a maraschino cherry, then serve.

Belle's Booze-less FRENCH 75

PREP: 5 min • COOK: 5 min • SERVES: 2

INGREDIENTS

8 ounces fresh lemon juice (from about 8 lemons)

3 ounces cucumber simple syrup (See recipe at right)

Club soda

Persian cucumber, thinly sliced lengthwise for garnish

DIRECTIONS

1 In a drink shaker, combine the lemon juice and cucumber syrup with ¼ cup ice. Shake to blend.

2 Fill two rock glasses halfway with ice and divide the cocktail evenly between the glasses. Top off with club soda, then garnish each with cucumber slices and serve.

Jack-Jack Strawberry MILK PUNCH

PREP: 5 min • COOK: 5 min • SERVES: 2

INGREDIENTS

2 cups oat milk

2 to 3 tablespoons honey

1 cup halved strawberries, plus 2 whole for garnish

DIRECTIONS

1 In a blender, combine the milk, 1 cup halved strawberries, and honey. Blend until smooth.

2 Evenly divide the punch between the glasses. Garnish each with a whole strawberry and serve.

Yeti's YELLOW LEMON SLUSH

PREP: 5 min • COOK: 5 min • SERVES: 2

INGREDIENTS

3 lemons, juiced, plus slices for garnish

4 ounces basil simple syrup (See recipe at right)

Basil sprigs, for garnish

DIRECTIONS

1 In a blender, combine the lemon juice, basil simple syrup, 1 cup water, and 2 cups ice. Blend until smooth.

2 Evenly divide the slush between two glasses. Garnish each with a lemon slice and sprig of basil, then serve.

SIMPLE SYRUP

In a saucepan over medium heat, combine 1 cup water with 1 cup sugar. Simmer until the sugar is dissolved, about 5 minutes. Let cool, then refrigerate in an airtight container until ready to use.

For cucumber syrup, combine the water and sugar with ½ an English cucumber and simmer as described above. Let steep 15 minutes, then cool and refrigerate.

For basil syrup, combine the water and sugar with 1 cup fresh basil leaves and simmer as described above. Let steep 15 minutes, then cool and refrigerate.

Arlo's KALE CHIPS

PREP
5 min

COOK
15 min

SERVES
4

Even if you're not a part of the **HEALTH FOOD** set, you'll be **TEMPTED** by these **DELICATE** veggie chips. To switch things up, we made our version with **DINOSAUR KALE**—a fitting variety for the recipe's **PREHISTORIC NAMESAKE**.

INGREDIENTS

1 large bunch lacinato kale, stemmed and torn into pieces

2 tablespoons olive oil

Kosher salt

DIRECTIONS

1 Heat the oven to 350°F. Use paper towels to pat dry the kale, then toss it in a large bowl with the olive oil.

2 Evenly divide the kale between two baking sheets and spread in an even layer. Bake until crisp, turning the pans halfway through, about 15 minutes. Sprinkle with salt and serve.

Helpful TIP

We like using lacinato (aka dinosaur) kale for this recipe for obvious reasons, but curly green kale is a tasty alternative. No matter which variety you choose, just be sure to keep an eye on the chips as they bake to avoid burning.

54   SIPS and SNACKS

Snowball ENERGY BITES

PREP
5 min

COOK
10 min

MAKES
About
1½ dozen

There's no added sugar in these all-natural truffles. Instead, they get their **SWEETNESS** from caramelly pitted dates and shredded **COCONUT**. Pack a few in your bag to keep you going on a long hike, or tuck a couple in your lunch bag for a midday **INDULGENCE**.

INGREDIENTS

1 cup roasted cashews

16 pitted dates

4 teaspoons chia seeds

1½ cups shredded unsweetened coconut

DIRECTIONS

1. In a food processor, combine the cashews, dates, and chia seeds with ½ cup coconut and 2 tablespoons water. Process until the mixture comes together and forms a ball.

2. Place the remaining coconut in a shallow bowl. Scoop a level tablespoon of the date mixture and roll into a ball. Coat with coconut and transfer to a plate. Repeat with the remaining mixture and coconut. Keep refrigerated until ready to eat.

Frozen Banana DALMATIAN POPS

PREP
5 min

COOK
3 hr 25 min
(includes
freezing time)

MAKES
8

Even **CRUELLA** might crack a smile at these spotted pops dipped in a **HOMEMADE** chocolate shell. Be sure to use coconut oil for the **RECIPE** and not another oil. The latter won't set properly.

INGREDIENTS

4 small bananas, halved crosswise

1 cup white chocolate chips

2 tablespoons coconut oil

⅓ cup dark chocolate chips

Special equipment
8 food-safe wooden treat sticks

DIRECTIONS

1 Line a small baking sheet with parchment paper. Insert a wooden treat stick into the flat side of each banana and place it on the sheet. Freeze the bananas until solid, about 3 hours.

2 Melt the white chocolate according to the package directions. Add the coconut oil and whisk until melted. Transfer to a mug or tall glass.

3 Dip each banana in the chocolate, letting the excess drip off, then return them to the baking sheet. Melt the chocolate chips according to the package directions. Place in a piping bag fit with an extra-small writing tip. Pipe spots onto each banana pop, then return the pops to the freezer until ready to serve. Like sprinkles, the spots pop off easily, so take care when eating!

Hidden Mickey APPLE SLICE SANDWICHES

PREP
5 min

COOK
10 min

SERVES
2

It's not hard to spot the **FAMOUS** pair of ears on this fruit snack that's perfect for a late-afternoon nosh. What's more, you don't need any **SPECIAL TOOLS** to create Mickey's shape—a mini round pastry cutter and a small round pastry tip (or drinking straw) will do.

INGREDIENTS

1 large apple

⅓ cup of your favorite nut butter

¼ cup crisp rice cereal or chopped almonds

DIRECTIONS

1 Cut the apple crosswise into ¼-inch-thick slices (you should have enough for 4 sandwiches). Remove the seeds. To form Mickey's head, use a mini round pastry cutter to cut a circle in the center of half the slices. Cut two small ears atop each head with the end of a round pastry tip.

2 Spread the remaining apple slices with a heaping tablespoon of nut butter so that it reaches the edges. Press a cut slice on top of each.

3 Place the rice cereal in a small bowl. Dip the edges of each sandwich in the cereal to coat the nut butter.

Helpful TIP

Add a nutritional boost to this snack by using brown rice cereal in place of conventional rice cereal.

SIPS and SNACKS · 61

Baymax COCOA

PREP
10 min

COOK
10 min

SERVES
2

The **HERO** that inspired this cozy recipe is cleverly made with **PILLOWY** marshmallows. We like the look (and taste) of melted **CHOCOLATE** for his face, but you can save some time by drawing it on with a **BLACK FOOD WRITER.**

INGREDIENTS

2 regular marshmallows

6 mini marshmallows

¼ cup chocolate chips

4 tablespoons unsweetened cocoa powder

4 tablespoons sugar

Pinch of salt

2 cups of your favorite milk

BAYMAX HOW-TO

DIRECTIONS

1 With kitchen shears, snip a slit on two sides of each regular marshmallow to form Baymax's arms, as shown. For the legs, snip a small piece from the end of 4 mini marshmallows. Attach a pair to each body by using the sticky end of each along with a dab of water.

2 Snip a small piece from the end of the two remaining mini marshmallows and use the sticky side and a dab of water to adhere it to the top of each body.

3 Melt the chocolate according to the package directions. Use a toothpick to apply chocolate eyes to each head, as shown. Set aside.

4 In a small saucepan over medium-low heat, whisk together the cocoa, sugar, salt, and 2 tablespoons milk. Warm until the cocoa and sugar are dissolved, then add the remaining milk and heat, whisking occasionally, until hot.

5 Evenly divide the cocoa between two mugs. Garnish each with a marshmallow Baymax and serve immediately.

POP STARS

MOVIE NIGHT REQUIRES THE PROPER PROVISIONS— most importantly, a tempting snack. These Disney-inspired popcorn mixes fit the bill, but beware: though each batch makes enough for a group, you'll likely want to keep the whole bowl for yourself.

FOR EACH COMBO, start with 8 cups of freshly popped plain popcorn and season with kosher salt to taste (we like to shake together the ingredients with the popcorn in a sealable bag). For popcorn with candy coatings, follow the package directions for melting, toss the popcorn in a bowl with the coating, then spread it on a parchment-lined baking sheet before sprinkling on additional toppings.

Snow White's
APPLE–CINNAMON POP

1½ cups chopped dried apples + ⅔ cup dried cranberries + ½ teaspoon cinnamon

Pooh's
HONEY–ALMOND POP

1⅓ cups melted butterscotch chips blended with 4 teaspoons melted coconut oil + 1 cup toasted sliced almonds + 4 cups honeycomb-shaped cereal

Dumbo's PB&J POP

1 tablespoon melted
coconut oil $+$ 2 tablespoons
powdered peanut butter
$+$ $2/3$ cup freeze-dried
strawberries

Rapunzel's ROYAL PURPLE POP

1 cup melted purple
candy melts
$+$ 3 tablespoons yellow
nonpareils

Peter Pan's GREEN-and-GOLD NEVER LAND POP

2 teaspoons olive oil
$+$ 5 teaspoons powdered
nutritional yeast
$+$ $1 1/2$ teaspoons dried dill
$+$ $1/4$ teaspoon garlic powder
$+$ $1/8$ teaspoon
smoked paprika

Lilo's Tropical FRUIT CONES with KAHLÚA DRIZZLE

PREP
10 min

COOK
15 min

MAKES
8

Forgoing the usual ice cream and sprinkles, we've **FILLED** and **TOPPED** these cones with more grown-up goodies. Fresh fruit is spooned into each, then **GENEROUSLY** dolloped with a Kahlúa cream that tastes like an **IRRESISTIBLE** slice of cheesecake. You can make the salad and topping ahead, but don't fill the cones until just before serving or they'll get soggy.

INGREDIENTS

2 kiwifruit, diced

1 cup pineapple, chopped

8 strawberries, quartered

½ mango, diced

½ cup Greek yogurt

½ cup sour cream

4 teaspoons Kahlúa liqueur

¼ cup light brown sugar

¼ teaspoon vanilla extract

8 waffle cones

¼ cup toasted coconut chips

8 maraschino cherries, for garnish (optional)

DIRECTIONS

1 In a small bowl, stir together the kiwifruit, pineapple, strawberries, and mango. Set aside. In another bowl, whisk together the yogurt, sour cream, Kahlúa, sugar, and vanilla.

2 Just before serving, evenly divide the fruit salad among the cones. Top each with a generous dollop of the Kahlúa cream, a sprinkle of coconut chips, and a cherry. Serve immediately.

Apricot CLOWN FISH

PREP
5 min

COOK
45 min
(includes cooling time)

MAKES
12

Reel in your **PARTY** guests with an under-the-sea-themed snack that resembles the characters **FEATURED** in *Finding Nemo* and *Finding Dory*. A two-step process and short list of ingredients make it **EASY** to scale up if you're feeding a crowd.

INGREDIENTS

18 dried apricots, cut crosswise into thirds

⅓ cup white candy melts

12 mini chocolate chips

DIRECTIONS

1 Line a baking sheet with parchment paper. Assemble each fish on the prepared sheet using four apricot pieces, as shown. Discard any extra pieces (you'll have 6 centers left over).

2 Melt the candy according to the package directions. Transfer to a small bowl. To assemble each fish, dip the cut end of the body pieces and the round edge of the tail piece in the chocolate and press the segments together, as shown. Use leftover chocolate to attach a chocolate-chip eye to each fish. Let the candy set before serving.

CLOWN FISH HOW-TO

Mini CHEESE BALL MICE

PREP 5 min

COOK 25 min

MAKES 12

Show off your garnishing **SKILLS** by filling your cheese board with a **CLEVERLY** assembled snack. Each cracker is a generous portion, so even a single batch will go a long way—**ESPECIALLY** when accompanied with other fresh fruits or veggies.

INGREDIENTS

1 small stalk celery

1 red baby bell pepper

4 black olives

8 ounces pub cheese

12 large water crackers

6 chives, halved

DIRECTIONS

1 Cut 24 thin slices from the celery stalk. Place on a plate and cover with a damp paper towel. Trim 12 noses from the baby bell pepper and 12 sets of eyes from the olives.

2 To assemble each mouse, shape a tablespoon-size portion of the pub cheese into a ball. Place on a cracker and add a chive tail, celery-slice ears, a bell-pepper nose, and olive eyes. Repeat with the remaining cheese and vegetables. Keep refrigerated until ready to serve.

Night Howler LEMONADE

PREP
5 min

COOK
3 hr 15 min
(includes freezing time)

SERVES
4

A dash of **UNEXPECTED COLOR**—inspired by the havoc-wreaking flower featured in *Zootopia*—can lend a **DRAMATIC** touch to a classic summer drink. Blend each glass with an equal amount of your favorite IPA for a simple and **REFRESHING** cocktail.

INGREDIENTS

4 cups of your favorite prepared lemonade (a light-colored drink works best), chilled

Blue food coloring

Lemon slices, for garnish

Special equipment
Star-shaped ice or food mold

DIRECTIONS

1. Fill the mold with water and freeze until solid, about 3 hours.

2. In a large pitcher, stir together the lemonade with 2 drops food coloring. If needed, add another drop or two to reach the desired hue.

3. Evenly divide the drink into glasses and add a few star ice cubes. Garnish with lemon slices and serve.

Honeybee MINES

PREP
5 min

COOK
35 min

MAKES
4 dozen

There's no mistaking Pooh's **FAVORITE** food, but if we had to guess his favorite flying creature we'd presume it was a bee. This **EDIBLE** version is a **TRIFECTA** of peanut butter, crispy rice cereal, and **CHOCOLATE**.

INGREDIENTS

½ cup creamy peanut butter

2 tablespoons honey

¼ cup butter, softened

½ cup confectioners' sugar, sifted

1¼ cups crisp rice cereal, crushed

⅓ cup dark chocolate chips

Sliced almonds

DIRECTIONS

1 In a large bowl, stir together the peanut butter, honey, and butter. Add the sugar and cereal, and stir until evenly blended and the mixture comes together into a shaggy dough.

2 Line a baking sheet with parchment paper. To shape each bee, roll a heaping tablespoon-size portion of the dough into a bee shape, as shown, and place on the prepared sheet. Repeat with the remaining dough, then place in the refrigerator to firm up the candies.

3 Melt the chocolate according to the package directions. Place the chocolate in a piping bag fit with a small writing tip. Pipe stripes onto each candy and add a pair of almond-slice wings. Keep refrigerated until ready to serve.

HONEYBEE HOW-TO

Mowgli's PAWPAW SMOOTHIE

PREP
5 min

COOK
5 min

SERVES
2

When they **SING** about "the bare necessities," Mowgli and Baloo name-drop a famously **SWEET** fruit called pawpaw—also known as papaya. It's combined here into a sip-worthy **TROPICAL** smoothie that also includes coconut, banana, and pineapple.

INGREDIENTS

2 cups ripe papaya, diced

1 frozen banana, broken into pieces

1 cup full-fat coconut milk

½ cup frozen pineapple chunks

1 tablespoon honey (optional)

Sliced star fruit, for garnish

DIRECTIONS

1 Combine all the ingredients in a blender and blend until smooth. Divide evenly between 2 glasses. Garnish with a slice of star fruit and serve immediately.

Ingredient SWAP

We chose full-fat milk for this recipe due to its creamy consistency, but you can sub in a lower-fat, coconut milk if you'd like. The result will be less rich (and also fewer calories!).

Stoplight CAPRESE SKEWERS

PREP
10 min

COOK
15 min

MAKES
12

An Italian salad on a stick? Yes, **PLEASE**! Tomatoes and melon may seem like an unlikely **COMBINATION**, but r est assured the ingredients offer just the right balance of **SAVORY** and **SWEET**.

INGREDIENTS

Small bunch fresh basil

12 cherry tomatoes

½ large cantaloupe, cut into balls

½ large honeydew, cut into balls

24 balls mini mozzarella

Olive oil, for drizzling

Balsamic vinegar, for drizzling

Kosher salt

Black pepper

Special equipment
9- to 10-inch skewers

DIRECTIONS

1 Remove the leaves from the basil stems. Assemble the skewers as shown, by threading 1 tomato, 1 ball of each melon, 2 mozzarella balls, and 3 basil leaves onto each stick. Arrange the skewers on a platter and refrigerate until ready to eat. Just before serving, drizzle with olive oil and balsamic vinegar, and season with salt and pepper.

Jasmine's GOLDEN LENTIL CRACKERS

PREP
5 min

COOK
45 min
(includes cooling time)

MAKES
About
5 dozen

These rustic crackers represent the **GLIMMERING** night sky that surrounds Jasmine as she takes her first trip on a **MAGIC CARPET** with Aladdin. Serve them with a spreadable cheese, hummus, or your **FAVORITE** savory spread.

INGREDIENTS

¾ cup yellow lentils

1 cup all-purpose flour

1 tablespoon sesame seeds

1 tablespoon cumin seeds

2½ teaspoons kosher salt

1½ teaspoons sugar

3 tablespoons olive oil

6 tablespoons water

Special equipment
Crescent cookie cutter

Star cookie cutter

DIRECTIONS

1. Heat oven to 400°F and line two baking sheets with parchment paper. Place the lentils in a high-powered blender and blend until the lentils are completely powdered. Transfer to a bowl.

2. Add the flour, sesame seeds, cumin seeds, salt, sugar, and olive oil to the bowl, along with 6 tablespoons water. Stir until evenly blended and the mixture has formed into a shaggy ball of dough. If the dough is too dry, add more water, 1 teaspoon at a time.

3. Roll out the dough as thin as possible and use the cookie cutters to shape it into stars and crescents. Arrange the crackers on the baking sheets. Gather and reroll the dough as needed.

4. Bake the crackers until they begin to brown slightly around the edges, about 8 minutes. Let cool completely before serving.

Where to BUY

If you don't have a high-powered blender, look for lentil flour at your local international food market. You'll need 1 scant cup for this recipe.

Chapter

3

SALADS, LUNCH, and LIGHT FARE

THE NEED FOR A MIDDAY REFUEL IS INEVITABLE.

So treat yourself to a homemade meal that will satisfy, whether at home with friends (see Alice's Teensy Tea Party Lunch, page 106) or on the go (see Lightning McQueen Bento, page 90). Most recipes in this chapter work best as afternoon fare, but many can also work as light and easy evening (or party) meal.

Pirate BENTO

PREP
15 min

COOK
5 min

SERVES
1

AHOY, MATEY! This all-veg lunch wouldn't last more than a day at sea, but it can satisfy afternoon **BELLY GRUMBLES**. In keeping with a Caribbean theme, we added tropical fruit sword skewers made with pineapple and mango for a naturally **SWEET TREAT**.

INGREDIENTS

1 slice cheddar cheese

1 slice provolone

2 slices whole wheat sandwich bread

1 Persian cucumber

3 tablespoons of your favorite hummus

1 small blueberry

6 (1-inch) cubes pineapple

6 (1-inch) cubes mango

1 medium purple carrot, peeled and sliced into ¼-inch-thick coins

¼ cup fish-shaped pretzels or crackers

Special equipment
Plastic sword picks

DIRECTIONS

1 Use a large round cookie cutter to cut a circle from the cheese and bread slices. Reserve the provolone scraps. Cut ¾ of the cucumber into ¼-inch-thick slices. Spread one side of each bread round with 1 tablespoon hummus, then sandwich the cucumber slices in between.

2 Attach the round of provolone to the top of the sandwich with dots of hummus. Cut away ⅓ of the cheddar round for the bandana and use the remaining piece to cut a small *V* for the knot. With the end of a drinking straw, cut polka dots and a nose from the provolone scraps. Attach the cheese pieces with the remaining hummus, as shown. (A toothpick works well for applying small dots.)

3 Cut the pirate's eye patch, mustache, and goatee from the peel of the remaining cucumber. Affix with hummus. Add the blueberry eye.

4 Thread the pineapple and mango onto plastic sword picks. Place the skewers, along with the carrots, pretzels or crackers, and sandwich, in a bento box. Keep cool until ready to eat.

Bambi BENTO

PREP
5 min

COOK
10 min

SERVES
1

We'll admit that throwing together a plain turkey sandwich is **SIMPLER** than making what's featured in this recipe. But it wouldn't be anything to **FAWN** over. Pulling off this sweet-looking **WOODLAND** meal requires just a few extra minutes, and it is **EASIER** to assemble than you might think!

INGREDIENTS

2 slices whole wheat bread

Mayonnaise or mustard, for spreading

2 slices deli turkey

1 slice your favorite cheese

3 blueberries

2 slices honeydew melon, cut ½-inch thick

2 tablespoons ranch dressing

¼ cup black olives

¼ cup bunny-shaped crackers

Special equipment
Butterfly-shaped cookie cutter

DIRECTIONS

1 With a sharp knife, cut the bread slices into the shape of Bambi's head, as shown (they should be identical). Reserve a 2-inch piece of crust. Spread one side of each bread slice with mayonnaise or mustard. Trim a slice of turkey and the cheese to fit in the bread, then sandwich them between the slices. Use a dab of mayonnaise or mustard to attach the crust at the top of the sandwich (trim if needed), as shown.

2 Cut the muzzle, eyes, and insides of the ears from the remaining slice of turkey. Attach with small dots of mayo, applied with a toothpick. Cut away a small piece from the bottom of each blueberry so it sits flat, then set them in place for the nose and pupils.

3 Use a mini butterfly cookie cutter to cut shapes from the melon slices. Place them in a well of a bento box. Fill a silicone baking cup with the dressing and place in another well, along with the olives and bunny-shaped crackers. Add the sandwich to the box to complete the bento. Keep cool until ready to eat.

Brave Bear BENTO

PREP
5 min

COOK
15 min

SERVES
1

When a witch's hex transforms Merida's mother into a **BEAR**, the princess realizes she's gotten more than what she **WISHED** for. Complete with pretzel-stick arrows, curly carrot ribbon salad, and a wild sandwich centerpiece, this **ENCHANTING** lunch will cast a **SPELL** of another kind—delight!

INGREDIENTS

For the bear sandwich

1 sandwich roll

⅓ cup prepared tuna salad (see Never Growing Up Tuna Sailboats, page 101)

1 slice white cheddar

2 round melba toasts

2 teaspoons mayonnaise

3 black olives

For the carrot salad

1 teaspoon honey

2 tablespoons olive oil

2 teaspoons red wine vinegar

2 tablespoons raisins

1 large carrot, cut into ribbons with a vegetable peeler

Kosher salt

For the arrows

3 ounces block cheddar

8 pretzel sticks

Half apple, sliced

DIRECTIONS

1 Sandwich the tuna salad inside the roll. For the ears, use a mini round cutter to shape three circles from the cheese slice. Adhere one to each melba toast with a dot of mayonnaise, then tuck the edge of each toast into the sandwich, as shown. Trim the ends of two olives for the eyes and halve the remaining olive to form a nose. Attach each along with the remaining cheese circle with mayonnaise. Cut a mouth from the remaining olive scraps and attach with more mayonnaise.

2 In a small bowl, whisk together the honey, olive oil, and red wine vinegar. Add the raisins and carrots and toss to coat. Season with salt.

3 Cut the cheddar into 8 small triangles. To assemble each arrow, use a skewer to bore a hole in the side of a cheese triangle, then insert the end of a pretzel. Repeat with the remaining pretzels and cheese.

4 Place the sandwich, salad, pretzel arrows, and apple slices into a bento box. Cover and keep cool until ready to eat.

Lightning McQueen BENTO

PREP
10 min

COOK
10 min

SERVES
1

A fresh fruit salad and a veggie-hummus sandwich place this Cars lunch **AHEAD** of the pack, and **CRUNCHY** traffic cones (corn snacks) and a set of edible tires (cookies) **ROUND** out the meal.

INGREDIENTS

For the car sandwich

½ small red bell pepper

¼ small yellow bell pepper

3 large black olives

3 tablespoons of your favorite hummus

1 thick slice whole grain bread, toasted

For the stoplight fruit salad

2 large strawberries, diced

¼ cup green grapes, halved

1 slice pineapple, cut into segments

2 round chocolate cookies

1 tablespoon vanilla frosting (optional)

½ cup cone-shaped corn snacks

DIRECTIONS

1 Trim the edges of the red bell pepper piece and cut a windshield and mouth into the center, as shown. Use a mini round cutter to shape two circles of yellow bell pepper, then trim a lightning bolt from the remaining piece. Trim an eye from each black olive and halve the remaining olive to form two wheels. Set aside a teaspoon of the hummus, then spread the remaining on the toasted bread and arrange the facial features and tires, as shown, using the extra hummus to attach the cheeks.

2 In a small bowl, toss together the fruit. If using frosting, add a dollop to each cookie tire.

3 Place the sandwich, fruit salad, cookies, and corn snacks in a bento. Cover and keep cool until ready to eat.

Ingredient SWAP

Red bell peppers and hummus are a perfect sandwich flavor match, but any bean—or even cream cheese—works as an alternative spread.

Olaf BENTO

PREP
5 min

COOK
15 min

SERVES
1

This **COOL HOMAGE** to Frozen's summer-loving snowman also features a nod to another character in the film—**SVEN**. The pretzels are meant to represent the **REINDEER'S ANTLERS**.

INGREDIENTS

2 (6-inch) flour tortillas

2 tablespoons cream cheese

1 slice deli ham

1 large black olive

1 rib celery

½ baby carrot

2 slices cantaloupe, cut ½-inch thick

1 slice watermelon, cut ½-inch thick

4 large pretzel twists

Special equipment
Mini flower cookie cutter

DIRECTIONS

1 Layer the tortillas, then use kitchen shears to cut them into the shape of Olaf's head, as shown. Cut the teeth from one of the scraps. Cut a slit in one of the tortilla heads with a sharp knife. Spread the other with 1 tablespoon cream cheese and layer on the ham. Sandwich with the slit tortilla.

2 Halve the olive. Use the end of a drinking straw to cut two pupils from one half. Trim two thin eyebrows from the other. Cut three thin strips of celery for Olaf's hair, as shown. Tuck the celery strips into the top of the sandwich. Roll two small balls of cream cheese and press them in place for the eyes, as shown. Add the olive pupils on top. Use more cream cheese to attach the eyebrows and a carrot nose (a toothpick works well for this task). Tuck the teeth inside Olaf's mouth and add a bit of cream cheese on top for color.

3 Use a mini flower-shaped cookie cutter to shape the melon slices. Cut out the center of each flower with a mini round cutter, then place the cut pieces in a flower with a contrasting color, as shown.

4 Break the pretzels into pieces so they resemble antlers. Place them in a bento box, along with the Olaf sandwich and melon flowers. Keep cool until ready to eat.

Aladdin's FATTOUSH SALAD

PREP
10 min

COOK
25 min

SERVES
6

The combination of **FRESH HERBS** and sumac—a crimson-colored spice ground from dried fruit—gives this popular **MIDDLE EASTERN** bread salad its bright, citrusy notes. You can find **SUMAC** at many conventional grocery stores and most international food markets.

INGREDIENTS

For the dressing

¼ cup fresh lemon juice

6 tablespoons olive oil

1 tablespoon ground sumac

1 teaspoon kosher salt

¼ teaspoon black pepper

For the salad

2 pitas, cut into 2-inch pieces

2 teaspoons olive oil

1 large head romaine lettuce, washed and torn into bite-size pieces

1 medium green bell pepper, chopped into ½-inch pieces

2 Roma tomatoes, seeded and chopped

3 Persian cucumbers, sliced

3 small radishes, sliced

2 scallions, finely sliced

⅓ cup chopped fresh parsley

¼ cup chopped fresh mint

DIRECTIONS

1 In a small bowl, combine all the ingredients for the dressing and whisk together vigorously.

2 Heat the oven to 400°F. Brush the pita with olive oil on both sides and arrange on a baking sheet. Toast in the oven, turning once, until crisp, about 8 minutes.

3 In a large bowl, combine the remaining salad ingredients. Add the pita chips and half the dressing. Toss to coat. Taste, and add more dressing if desired. Serve immediately.

Crystal Palace PASTA SALAD

PREP
10 min

COOK
20 min

SERVES
6

Named after the restaurant in the **MAGIC KINGDOM** where it's served, this colorful, **VEGGIE-PACKED** pasta dish comes straight from the chef's repertoire. It's incredibly tasty as is, but you can put your own culinary spin on it by **SWAPPING VEGGIES** or herbs, or even adding your favorite diced salami.

INGREDIENTS

1 pound penne pasta

½ cup roughly chopped kalamata olives

¼ cup thinly sliced red onions

½ cup thinly sliced red bell peppers

½ cup thinly sliced green bell peppers

⅔ cup halved cherry tomatoes

⅓ cup white balsamic vinegar

⅔ cup olive oil

2 tablespoons chopped fresh chives

Kosher salt

Black pepper

½ cup crumbled feta

½ cup shredded Parmesan

DIRECTIONS

1 Cook the pasta according to the package directions. Drain and rinse in cool water, then transfer to a large bowl and toss with the olives, onions, bell peppers, and tomatoes.

2 In a small bowl, whisk together vinegar, olive oil, and chives. Season to taste with salt and pepper. Pour half the dressing over the pasta mixture and toss to coat. Fold in the feta and Parmesan. Add more dressing and season to taste if desired. Chill until ready to serve.

Helpful TIP

Using shaker Parmesan is convenient but won't yield the same delicious results as shredding it yourself. If you're still not up to the task, look for pre-shredded Parmesan in the cheese section of your grocery store.

Mrs. Potts MELON SALAD

PREP
10 min

COOK
20 min

SERVES
6

Turn **ORDINARY** fruit into an **EXTRAORDINARY** edible object with just a few fancy cuts. Serve it as the **CENTERPIECE** to an easygoing brunch or (you guessed it!) afternoon tea.

INGREDIENTS

1 whole cantaloupe

½ cup blueberries

1 large strawberry

1 tablespoon honey

1 cup watermelon balls

Special equipment

Melon baller

Toothpicks

TRIMMING FRUIT HOW-TO

TOOTHPICKS HOW-TO

DIRECTIONS

1 Trim 2 inches from the stem end of the cantaloupe and 1 inch from the opposite end. Halve the 2-inch piece crosswise, then cut a spout and handle from the flat portion as shown. Set all the pieces aside.

2 Scrape the seeds from the cantaloupe. Leaving the outside of the fruit intact, use a melon baller to cut the flesh and transfer to a bowl.

3 Set the empty melon atop the remaining flat melon slice. Secure it in place from the inside with toothpicks, as shown. Use more toothpicks to attach the spout, handle, and two blueberry eyes. (Break the toothpicks into shorter pieces if they are too long.)

4 Trim and reserve the top of the strawberry, then cut the remaining piece into thin slices. Trim one slice into eyebrows and a mouth, as shown. Halve the remaining slices crosswise. Use a dab of honey applied with a toothpick to attach the eyebrows and mouth to the face, and the pieces around the bottom edge of the teapot, as shown. Thread a blueberry and the strawberry top onto a toothpick, then insert it into the center of the remaining cantaloupe slice, as shown, for the pot lid.

5 Fill the cantaloupe pot with the remaining berries and cut fruit. Top with the lid. Keep chilled until ready to serve.

Never Growing Up TUNA SAILBOATS

PREP
10 min

COOK
20 min

SERVES
4 to 6

In a **MISCHIEVOUS** culinary twist, a very grown-up salad is **DISGUISED** as a youthful dish by serving it in little bell pepper boats. But don't be fooled! Fresh dill, roasted peppers, and almonds (trust us, you'll love the **CRUNCH**!) make this version of tuna altogether adult-ish—just don't tell Peter Pan.

INGREDIENTS

1 (7-ounce) jar tuna packed in oil

4 teaspoons toasted slivered almonds, roughly chopped

2 small stalks celery, sliced

2 tablespoons chopped roasted red bell pepper

2 tablespoons minced fresh dill

¼ cup mayonnaise

Kosher salt

Black pepper

6 to 8 baby bell peppers, halved and seeded

6 leaves romaine lettuce

Special equipment
12 to 16 (4-inch) bamboo skewers or toothpicks

DIRECTIONS

1 In a medium bowl, combine the tuna, almonds, celery, roasted red bell pepper, dill, and mayonnaise. Season with salt and pepper to taste.

2 Trim a small slice from the bottom of each bell pepper half so that it sits flat, as shown, being careful not to cut a hole all the way through. Trim the lettuce into sails for each boat, then thread each leaf onto a skewer, as shown. Spoon a portion of tuna salad into each bell pepper and finish with a lettuce sail. Refrigerate until ready to serve.

CUTTING THE PEPPERS HOW-TO

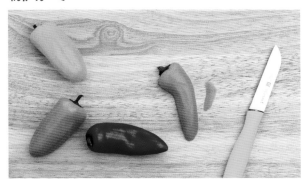

Dumbo's PEANUT ZOODLES

PREP
20 min

COOK
5 min

SERVES
4

While it's **SAFE** to assume this dish would never be fed to a real-life pachyderm, it earns its place in this collection by **FEATURING** the favorite snack of a fictitious one. Zucchini noodles are **DRESSED** in a peanut sauce that's at once sweet and **SPICY**. It's a no-cook meal with a **KICK**.

INGREDIENTS

For the peanut sauce

½ cup creamy peanut butter

1 tablespoon rice vinegar

1 tablespoon soy sauce

1 teaspoon sriracha

Juice and zest of a lime

1 tablespoon brown sugar

1-inch piece fresh ginger, grated

1 clove fresh garlic, grated

Black pepper

Kosher salt

For the zoodles

3 medium zucchini, trimmed and spiralized

1 large carrot cut into matchsticks

2 cups shredded red cabbage

¼ cup chopped peanuts, for garnish

¼ cup chopped cilantro, for garnish

DIRECTIONS

1 In a large bowl, whisk together the peanut butter, rice vinegar, soy sauce, sriracha, lime zest and juice, brown sugar, ginger, and garlic with ½ cup hot water until smooth. Season with salt and pepper to taste.

2 Add the zucchini, carrot, and cabbage to the sauce and toss to coat. Keep refrigerated until ready to serve topped with the peanuts and cilantro.

Ingredient SWAP

For a more filling main dish, try adding shredded chicken or fried tofu to these zoodles.

Jessie's Cowgirl SALAD with CORN BREAD CROUTONS

PREP
15 min

COOK
1 hr
(includes cooling time)

SERVES
6

A **SMOKY** tomato vinaigrette lends a southwest **TWANG** to this salad made with sweet corn, black beans, and avocado. The addition of corn bread croutons and a **SPRINKLE** of queso blanco turns it into a surprisingly filling main course.

INGREDIENTS

For the salad and croutons

1 (8-ounce) box corn bread mix

3 tablespoons melted butter

1 (15-ounce) can black beans, rinsed and drained

¾ cup grape tomatoes, halved

¼ cup sliced red onion

1½ cups fresh corn kernels

6 cups romaine lettuce, torn into bite-size pieces

⅓ cup cilantro leaves

1 ripe avocado, peeled and sliced

4 ounces queso blanco, crumbled

For the dressing

1 large ripe red tomato, roughly chopped (about 2 cups)

1 medium clove garlic, grated

1¼ teaspoons smoked paprika

¼ teaspoon chipotle chili powder

½ cup plus 2 tablespoons olive oil

2 tablespoons red wine vinegar

1½ teaspoons dried oregano

1 teaspoon kosher salt

DIRECTIONS

1. Prepare the corn bread in an 8-inch square baking dish according to the package directions. Let cool 15 minutes, then cut into 1-inch cubes and arrange on a baking sheet.

2. While the corn bread cools, prepare the dressing. Place all the ingredients in a small bowl. Use an immersion blender to puree the ingredients until smooth. Taste, adjust seasoning if desired, and blend once more to incorporate.

3. Adjust the oven temperature to 400°F. Brush the corn bread cubes with the melted butter, turning to coat each side. Bake until golden brown and crisp, turning halfway through, about 12 minutes. Let cool.

4. In a large bowl, toss together the black beans, tomatoes, onion, corn, romaine, and cilantro.

5. Before serving, top the salad with the avocado, queso, and corn bread croutons and drizzle with dressing.

Alice's Teensy TEA PARTY LUNCH

White Rabbit's Petite Pocket Watch Cookies (page 109)

Little London Fogs (page 108)

This DIMINUTIVE spread of both sweet and savory delights recall some of the most MEMORABLE scenes and characters from Alice's Wonderland ADVENTURES. You can play up the theme of tiny eats by serving guests these offerings on TEACUP SAUCERS and using cocktail forks.

Dainty Queen of Hearts Tomato Tarts (page 108)

Wee Strawberry Scones (page 109)

Mini Mad Hatter Tea Sandwiches (page 108)

Dainty Queen of Hearts TOMATO TARTS

PREP: 10 min • COOK: 30 min • MAKES: 18

INGREDIENTS

2 teaspoons olive oil

1 small leek, white and pale-green parts only, finely chopped

½ cup grape tomatoes, chopped

2 teaspoons chopped fresh basil

¼ teaspoon kosher salt

¼ teaspoon black pepper

1 refrigerated piecrust from a 15-ounce package

2 ounces goat cheese

1 egg

DIRECTIONS

1 Heat the oven to 400°F. In a small skillet over medium heat, warm the olive oil. Add the leek and cook until tender, about 5 minutes. Place in a small bowl and combine with the tomatoes, basil, salt, and pepper. Set aside.

2 Use a 2½-inch round cookie cutter to shape 18 circles from the piecrust dough, then shape 18 hearts from the remaining scraps with a mini heart cutter. When needed, gather and reroll the dough to ¼-inch thickness as you work.

3 Use a pastry tamper to mold each dough round in a well of a mini cupcake pan. Evenly divide the goat cheese among the tarts, followed by the tomato mixture. Top each tart with a dough heart.

4 In a small bowl, whisk the egg with 1 tablespoon water. Brush the tarts with the egg wash, then bake until light golden brown, about 12 minutes. Serve warm.

Little LONDON FOGS

PREP: 5 min • COOK: 10 min • SERVES: 2

INGREDIENTS

1 cup whole milk

2 sachets Earl Grey tea

4 teaspoons lavender syrup

¼ teaspoon vanilla extract

DIRECTIONS

1 In a small saucepan over medium heat, bring the milk and 1 cup of water to a simmer. Turn off the heat, add the tea bags, and steep 5 minutes.

2 Stir in the lavender and vanilla. Evenly divide between two teacups and drink immediately.

Mini Mad Hatter TEA SANDWICHES

PREP: 5 min • COOK: 20 min • MAKES: 12

INGREDIENTS

6 ounces cream cheese, at room temperature

4 teaspoons chopped fresh dill

¼ teaspoon lemon zest

Kosher salt

Black pepper

3 Persian cucumbers

24 slices cocktail bread

DIRECTIONS

1 In a small bowl, stir together the cream cheese, dill, and lemon zest. Season with salt and pepper. Use a vegetable peeler to cut thin ribbons of cucumber. Trim the pieces to fit the cocktail bread.

2 To make each sandwich, spread a slice of cocktail bread with 1½ teaspoons of the cream cheese mixture. Layer on strips of cucumber. Trim away the crust and halve on the diagonal. Repeat with the remaining ingredients. Keep chilled until ready to serve.

White Rabbit's Petite POCKET WATCH COOKIES

PREP: 5 min • COOK: 1 hr 15 min (includes cooling time)
MAKES: About 2½ dozen

INGREDIENTS

½ (16-ounce) roll store-bought sugar cookie dough, softened

2 tablespoons flour, plus more for dusting

1½ cups white frosting

Red food coloring

Yellow jelly beans

Chocolate sprinkles

DIRECTIONS

1 Heat the oven to 350°F and line 2 baking sheets with parchment paper. Knead together the cookie dough and flour, then roll it out to a ¼-inch thickness. Use a 2-inch round cutter to shape the dough into circles, and arrange them 2 inches apart on each baking sheet. Gather and reroll the dough as needed.

2 Place the cookies in the freezer for 10 minutes (this will help prevent too much spreading when they bake), then transfer to the oven and bake until light golden around the edges, about 12 minutes. Transfer to a rack to cool completely.

3 Place ¼ cup frosting in a small bowl and tint with red food coloring. Transfer to a piping bag fit with a small writing tip.

4 Working with one cookie at a time, use the white frosting to attach a jelly bean along the edge, as shown. Cover the center of the cookie with more frosting, and add 12 chocolate sprinkle numbers. Finish with red frosting clock hands. Repeat with the remaining cookies.

Wee STRAWBERRY SCONES

PREP: 10 min • COOK: 40 min • MAKES: 3 dozen

INGREDIENTS

For the scones

2 cups all-purpose flour, plus more for dusting

¼ teaspoon kosher salt

2 teaspoons baking powder

¼ teaspoon baking soda

⅓ cup sugar

½ cup (1 stick) cold unsalted butter, cut into small dice

1 cup chopped strawberries

½ cup plus 2 tablespoons heavy cream

For the lemon glaze

1½ cups confectioners' sugar

¼ teaspoon lemon zest

3 tablespoons lemon juice

¼ teaspoon vanilla

DIRECTIONS

1 Heat the oven to 350°F and line a baking sheet with parchment paper. In a large bowl, stir together the flour, salt, baking powder, baking soda, and sugar. Use a pastry blender to cut in the butter.

2 Stir in the strawberries until coated, then stir in the heavy cream. Gently work the dough until it holds together (it will be slightly dry). If the dough is too dry, add more cream one tablespoon at a time.

3 Turn the dough out onto a lightly floured surface. Dust your hands with flour and gently knead a few more times. Pat it into a ½-inch-thick rectangle, use a 1½-inch round cookie cutter to shape the dough into scones, then space them 1 inch apart on the baking sheet. Freeze 15 minutes.

4 Bake the scones until they're golden brown, turning halfway through, about 20 minutes. Let cool.

5 In a small bowl, stir together all the ingredients for the glaze, then drizzle over the scones. Let the glaze set before serving.

Luigi's HOT DOG DIPPERS

PREP
10 min

COOK
1 hr 40 min
(includes rising time)

MAKES
3 dozen

In keeping with Radiator Springs resident **LUIGI'S** love for all things Italian, this version of **PIGS IN A BLANKET** replaces store-bought crescent rolls with homemade pizza dough. The result is a more savory—and some might argue **SUPERIOR**—version of a **HARD-TO-RESIST** snack.

INGREDIENTS

4 teaspoons active dry yeast

1 teaspoon granulated sugar

1¼ cups warm water (110°F)

4 cups all-purpose flour, plus more for dusting

1½ teaspoons kosher salt

¼ cup light brown sugar

1 tablespoon olive oil

12 of your favorite hot dogs

1 egg

Sesame or poppy seeds

DIRECTIONS

1 In a small bowl, stir together the yeast, granulated sugar, and water. Let sit until foamy, about 10 minutes.

2 Meanwhile, in a medium bowl, whisk together the flour, salt, and brown sugar. Make a well in the center and add the yeast mixture. With a wooden spoon, gradually combine the wet and dry ingredients into a shaggy dough. If the mixture is too wet, add a few tablespoons of flour.

3 Turn the dough out onto a lightly floured surface and knead until it's smooth and elastic, about 10 minutes. Grease a large bowl with the oil, then add the dough and turn to coat. Cover with plastic wrap and let rise in a warm spot until doubled in size, about 1 hour.

4 Heat the oven to 450°F. Line two baking sheets with parchment paper. Cut the hot dogs into 2-inch-long portions.

5 Punch down the dough and evenly divide it into 12 portions. Roll each into a 12-inch-long rope, then cut it into 4-inch lengths. Wrap each hot dog in a portion of dough and place it seam side down on a baking sheet, spacing them 2 inches apart.

6 In a small bowl, whisk the egg with 1 tablespoon water. Use a pastry brush to coat the top of each dipper with the egg wash, then sprinkle it with sesame (or poppy) seeds. Bake until the dough is golden brown, about 8 minutes. Serve immediately.

Pinocchio Veggie BAGEL BITES

PREP
5 min

COOK
25 min

MAKES
6

WHITTLING the veggie details for each of these bagels will take a bit of patience, but the playful **EMBELLISHMENTS** are sure to bring a lunchtime gathering to **LIFE**!

INGREDIENTS

6 mini bagels

4 ounces cream cheese

1 Persian cucumber, thinly sliced

6 baby carrots

12 black olives

1 red baby bell pepper

3 baby radishes, thinly sliced

3 yellow baby bell peppers

DIRECTIONS

1 Spread one half of each bagel with 1 tablespoon cream cheese. Top with a single layer of cucumber slices, letting two hang over the edge to form ears, as shown. Sandwich each with a bagel top and insert a baby carrot nose in the center.

2 Trim an eye from each olive. Roll 12 small dots of cream cheese into balls, then use them to attach two olive eyes to each bagel. Cut three thin slices from the red bell pepper and halve them. Use more cream cheese to attach two radish cheeks and a red bell pepper mouth to each bagel.

3 Halve each yellow bell pepper lengthwise. Trim away a portion of the curved end of each to form a hat shape, as shown. Cut strips from the pepper scraps for each brim. Attach a bell pepper hat and brim to each bagel with cream cheese. (You can also skip attaching the hats and just set them in place on your serving platter.) Keep chilled until ready to serve.

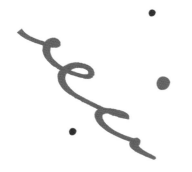

Tiana's SHRIMP and REMOULADE

PREP
5 min

COOK
25 min

SERVES
5

If you've ever eaten an authentic Louisiana po' boy, then you're likely familiar with the **DELICIOUSNESS** that is remoulade. Often its drizzled or **POURED** on sandwiches, but the zesty mayo-based condiment can also be used as a dip. Here it's served alongside boiled shrimp, and once you've tried it, you may **NEVER** go back to cocktail sauce.

INGREDIENTS

For the remoulade
¾ cup mayonnaise

2 tablespoons ketchup

1 tablespoon brown mustard

1½ teaspoons Tabasco

2 teaspoons Worcestershire sauce

1 teaspoon prepared horseradish

4 teaspoons chopped parsley

4 teaspoons capers, finely chopped

1 teaspoon grated garlic

Juice and zest of ½ lemon

1 teaspoon kosher salt

1¼ teaspoons creole seasoning

1 tablespoon chives

Black pepper, to taste

For the shrimp
3 stalks celery, sliced

2 carrots, sliced

4 cloves garlic, smashed

2 sprigs fresh thyme

1 small lemon, halved

1 pound jumbo shrimp, shell on

DIRECTIONS

1. In a small bowl, whisk together all the ingredients for the remoulade. Taste and adjust seasoning as desired. Cover and set aside to let the flavors meld.

2. In a large pot, combine the celery, carrots, garlic, thyme, and half the lemon with 2 quarts water. Bring to a boil.

3. Prepare an ice bath in a large bowl. Place the shrimp in the boiling water and let cook until pink, about 3 minutes. Transfer immediately to the ice bath, cool 5 minutes, then pat dry, arrange on a platter, and refrigerate until ready to serve. If you like, you can peel the shrimp before plating.

4. Squeeze the remaining lemon half over the shrimp and serve with the remoulade on the side.

Mumbai-Style Grilled VEGGIE SANDWICH

PREP
5 min

COOK
25 min

SERVES
4

This spicy, **TOASTED** sandwich doesn't call for any cheese, but you won't miss it. Inspired by a popular snack sold on the streets of Mumbai, it's **BURSTING** with **FLAVOR** from an herby chutney and a blend of peppery, aromatic **SPICES** called sandwich masala.

INGREDIENTS

For the green chutney

1¼ cups fresh cilantro

½ cup fresh mint

¼ small jalapeños

½-inch piece ginger, chopped

Juice and zest of 1 lime

2 cloves garlic, pressed

½ cup canola oil

½ teaspoon kosher salt

For the sandwich

8 slices sourdough bread

2 tablespoons butter, softened

2 large russet potatoes, boiled and sliced into ½-inch-thick rounds

¼ English cucumber, sliced

½ small red onion, sliced

1 large red tomato, sliced

Sandwich or chaat masala

DIRECTIONS

1 Place all the ingredients for the chutney in a blender or food processor and pulse to blend.

2 Spread one side of each bread slice with butter and the opposite side with chutney. With the chutney side up, layer one quarter each of the potato, cucumber, red onion, and tomato onto 4 of the slices. Sprinkle each generously with the sandwich masala, then top, buttered side up, with another slice of bread.

3 Warm a large skillet over medium heat. Add a sandwich and cook until golden and toasted, about 4 minutes per side. Repeat with the remaining sandwiches. Serve immediately.

Where to BUY

It's likely that you won't find sandwich masala at your local grocery store. Look for it at an Asian market or wherever global ingredients are sold in your area.

Chapter

4

PLAYFUL DINNERS

ADORNED WITH FRIENDLY FACES AND WHIMSICAL SHAPES, THESE RECIPES ADD A BIT OF DISNEY MAGIC TO IRRESISTIBLE EVERYDAY MEALS.

Easy yet unexpected, each dish is sure to put a smile on the face of everyone sitting at the dinner table.

Punk Rock Pink ANIMAL PASTA

PREP
15 min

COOK
30 min

SERVES
2

The **WILDLY** vibrant hue of this noodle dish doesn't come from a bottle. It's actually the result of a **RICH SAUCE** made with fresh beets and ricotta cheese. The recipe yields enough for two, but the second serving also makes a nice leftovers lunch—**HOT OR COLD.**

INGREDIENTS

For the beet sauce
2 medium red beets, peeled and quartered

1 tablespoon olive oil

½ small yellow onion, thinly sliced

¼ teaspoon salt, plus more for seasoning

2 tablespoons ricotta cheese

Black pepper

For the pasta
2 cups cooked spaghetti

8-ounce ball fresh mozzarella

4 pitted black olives

Handful fresh Italian parsley

2 cherry tomatoes

2 slices yellow bell pepper

DIRECTIONS

1 Fill a medium saucepan with water. Add the beets and bring to a boil. Reduce the heat to low and simmer until the beets are tender, about 20 minutes. Drain and let cool.

2 Meanwhile, in a small skillet over medium heat, warm the oil. Add the onion and salt, then cook until the onions are soft and light golden, about 10 minutes.

3 Combine the beets, onions, and ricotta in a food processor. Process until smooth, about 1 minute. Season to taste with salt and pepper.

4 In a medium skillet over low heat, toss together the pasta and beet sauce. Cook, stirring constantly, until heated through. Evenly divide the pasta between two plates.

5 Cut 4 slices from the mozzarella and use the remaining cheese to make teeth. Trim a circle from the end of each olive for the pupils. To create each face, arrange parsley leaf eyebrows on each portion of pasta, as shown. Layer on mozzarella slice eyes topped with olive pupils. Set a cherry tomato nose below the eyes. Finish each face by adding a bell pepper mouth and mozzarella teeth. Serve immediately.

Magic Carpet FLATBREAD

PREP
5 min

COOK
25 min

SERVES
8

Put a whole **NEW TWIST** on pizza night with this tasty *Aladdin*-inspired flatbread. Start with a base made of hummus in place of tomato sauce, then top with **WARM FALAFEL**, olives, **FRESH VEGGIES**, and feta—like a wish come true!

INGREDIENTS

1 sleeve refrigerated pizza dough

Flour, for dusting

1 cup hummus

6 pieces store-bought falafel

⅓ cup kalamata olives

½ cup grape tomatoes, halved

⅓ cup sliced banana peppers

⅓ cup crumbled feta

2 tablespoons chopped fresh parsley

DIRECTIONS

1 On a lightly floured surface, roll out the dough into a long rectangle. Use kitchen shears to fringe each end, as shown.

2 Fully bake the dough according to the package directions. Let cool slightly.

3 Spread the hummus onto the dough. Create a pattern on top with the falafel, olives, tomatoes, and peppers. Return to the oven to warm through, about 5 minutes, then garnish with the feta and parsley. Serve immediately.

DOUGH AND TASSELS HOW-TO

All SOUPED UP

Few things feel better than SNUGGLING UP with WARM SOUP on a cool night or whenever you're in need of a small cup of COMFORT. This trio of recipes offers a range of flavors in just a HANDFUL OF STEPS you can even achieve on a busy weeknight.

Mike Wazowski
Bowl-o-Broc
(page 126)

Woody's
Cowboy Chili
(page 127)

Tink's Chicken
and Stars
(page 126)

Mike Wazowski BOWL-O-BROC

PREP: 10 min • COOK: 35 min • SERVES: 6

INGREDIENTS

1 tablespoon olive oil

1 large onion, chopped

2 garlic cloves, minced

1 teaspoon kosher salt

½ teaspoon black pepper

8 cups broccoli florets from 2 small crowns

1 tablespoon sherry vinegar

6 cups chicken broth

1 large russet potato, peeled and diced

1 cup shredded cheddar

¼ cup grated Parmesan

9 slices white cheddar

1 green bell pepper

6 black olives

DIRECTIONS

1 In a large pot over medium heat, warm the oil. Add the onion and cook until softened, about 5 minutes. Add the garlic, salt, and pepper, and cook until fragrant, about 1 minute. Add half the broccoli and the sherry vinegar, and cook 3 minutes.

2 Pour in the broth and bring to a boil. Reduce to a simmer and add the potato and remaining broccoli. Cook until the vegetables are tender, about 10 minutes. Stir in the shredded cheddar and Parmesan. Remove from the heat and use an immersion blender to puree the soup.

3 Use a large round cookie cutter to shape 6 of the cheddar slices into circles. Use a slightly smaller round cutter to shape the bell pepper into 6 circles. Trim the remaining cheese slices into 12 horns. Trim a circle from the end of each olive.

4 To serve, ladle the soup into bowls. Top each with a round of cheddar, followed by a bell pepper eye and olive pupil. Finish with a pair of cheddar horns. Serve immediately.

Tink's CHICKEN and STARS

PREP: 10 min • COOK: 30 min • SERVES: 6

INGREDIENTS

2 tablespoons olive oil

2 celery stalks, sliced

2 medium carrots, peeled and diced

1 large onion, diced

2 garlic cloves, minced

½ teaspoon kosher salt

¼ teaspoon black pepper

6 cups chicken broth

½ teaspoon lemon zest

1 pound boneless, skinless chicken breast

⅓ cup pastina or stelline pasta

1 tablespoon chopped fresh dill

DIRECTIONS

1 In a large pot over medium heat, warm the oil. Add the celery, carrot, and onion, and cook until the vegetables are soft, about 5 minutes. Stir in the garlic, salt, and pepper, and cook until fragrant, about 1 minute. Add the broth and lemon zest, and bring to a boil. Add the chicken, reduce the heat to low, and simmer until the chicken is cooked through, about 10 minutes. Once cooked, transfer the chicken to a plate.

2 Add the pasta to the pot and cook until al dente, about 5 minutes. Shred the chicken into bite-size pieces, then return to the pot. Stir in the dill. Serve immediately.

Woody's COWBOY CHILI

PREP: 10 min • COOK: 45 min • SERVES: 8

INGREDIENTS

3 tablespoons olive oil

1 large green bell pepper, chopped

1 large onion, chopped

3 garlic cloves, minced

1 teaspoon dried oregano

1 tablespoon ground cumin

2 tablespoons chili powder

$\frac{1}{8}$ teaspoon chipotle chili powder

1 teaspoon kosher salt

$\frac{1}{2}$ teaspoon black pepper

1 pound ground turkey

1 (28-ounce) can whole tomatoes

1 cup tomato sauce

$1\frac{1}{2}$ cups chicken broth

$1\frac{1}{2}$ cups frozen corn

1 (15-ounce) can kidney beans

3 (6-inch) corn tortillas

Sour cream, sliced jalapeños, and cilantro for topping

Special equipment
Cowboy-hat cookie cutter

DIRECTIONS

1 In a large pot over medium heat, warm 2 tablespoons olive oil. Add the bell pepper and onion and cook until softened, about 5 minutes. Stir in the garlic, oregano, cumin, chili powders, salt, and pepper, and cook until fragrant, about 1 minute. Add the ground turkey and cook until no longer pink, using a wooden spoon to break it into small pieces as it browns, about 5 minutes.

2 Use your hand to break the tomatoes into pieces and add them to the pot with their juices. Stir in the tomato sauce, broth, corn, and kidney beans. Bring the chili to a boil. Reduce the heat to low and simmer uncovered, stirring occasionally, until thickened slightly, about 25 minutes.

3 Meanwhile, heat the oven to 350°F. Use the cowboy hat cutter to shape 3 hats from each tortilla. Brush both sides of each hat with the remaining olive oil. Arrange them on a baking sheet and bake until crisp, turning halfway through, about 8 minutes.

4 Ladle the chili into bowls, add a dollop of sour cream, and top with a tortilla hat. Finish with a scattering of jalapeños and cilantro. Serve immediately.

Aristocat-ic QUICHE MARIE

PREP
5 min

COOK
55 min

SERVES
8

We're sure **KITTEN MARIE** would say, *"Oui, oui!"* to this savory pie—and not just because it's styled in her likeness. The filling is based on a classic French recipe called **QUICHE LORRAINE**, which features a combination of bacon, scallions, and Jarlsberg cheese. **IRRESISTIBLE** indeed!

INGREDIENTS

Cooking spray

1 store-bought refrigerated piecrust

3 scallions, chopped

5 slices cooked bacon, chopped

¾ cup shredded Jarlsberg cheese

6 large eggs

1¼ cups heavy cream

¼ teaspoon kosher salt

⅛ teaspoon black pepper

Pinch ground nutmeg

2 large black olives, halved lengthwise

¼ small red bell pepper

½ small yellow bell pepper

9 fresh chives

2 slices white cheddar

DIRECTIONS

1 Heat the oven to 350°F. Coat a 9-inch pie pan with cooking spray. Place the piecrust in the pan and crimp the edges. Scatter the scallions, bacon, and cheese in the crust and toss lightly.

2 In a medium bowl, whisk together the eggs, heavy cream, salt, pepper, and nutmeg. Pour the mixture over the other filling ingredients. Bake until the filling is set in the center and beginning to brown in some spots, about 40 minutes. Let cool slightly.

3 To make Marie's face, slice an olive half into strips for the mouth. Halve the remaining olive to form two pupils. Cut a bow and nose from the red bell pepper and two ears from the yellow bell pepper. Trim 6 chives for the whiskers and 3 for the tuft of fur. Use a round cutter to cut a circle from each slice of cheddar for the eyes. Set all the pieces in place as shown. Serve immediately.

Helpful TIP

For a quick, time-saving riff on this recipe, replace the bacon with diced deli ham and use your favorite pre-shredded cheese in place of the Jarlsberg.

Mickey's TURKEY MEAT LOAF

PREP
10 min

COOK
45 min

SERVES
6

Making individual **MINI LOAVES** with this recipe has obvious appeal, but if you lack the time (or patience) to shape multiple portions, you can also mold the meat into **ONE LARGE LOG.** To cook, double the baking time.

INGREDIENTS

Cooking spray

3 eggs, lightly beaten

½ cup ketchup

¼ cup bulgur

2 tablespoons Worcestershire sauce

2 pounds ground turkey

2 small carrots, finely shredded

¼ cup finely diced red bell pepper

¼ cup finely diced yellow onion

2 teaspoons garlic powder

1 teaspoon onion powder

1 teaspoon kosher salt

½ teaspoon black pepper

DIRECTIONS

1 Heat oven to 400°F. Line two baking sheets with foil and coat with cooking spray. In a medium bowl, stir together the eggs, ketchup, bulgur, and Worcestershire sauce. Let sit 30 minutes.

2 Place ground turkey in a large bowl and use your hands to break it into pieces. Add the carrot, bell pepper, onion, garlic powder, onion powder, salt, pepper, and egg mixture. Mix with your hands until well combined.

3 Evenly divide mixture into 6 portions. Form each into a Mickey Mouse shape on the prepared sheet pans, spacing them 1 inch apart. Bake until the internal temperature reaches 165°F, about 22 minutes. Let rest 5 minutes, then serve.

Helpful TIP

This recipe can also be made with ground chicken. Just be sure to opt for meat that is all or mostly dark so that the end result isn't too dry.

Pascal's Green FARRO RISOTTO

PREP 5 min

COOK 50 min

SERVES 4

A cute chameleon's face isn't the only thing **CAMOUFLAGING** this hearty bowl. The green color comes from a pesto made with **PEPPERY** arugula, smoked almonds, and a hint of lemon. It's best served right away, but if you're planning to reheat it later, stir in a few **SPLASHES** of broth when you warm it to revive its creamy texture.

INGREDIENTS

½ cup smoked almonds

6 garlic cloves, minced

4 cups packed baby arugula

Juice of ½ a lemon

3 tablespoons grated Parmesan

Black pepper

½ cup plus 2 tablespoons olive oil

Kosher salt

8 black olives

1 large green bell pepper, quartered lengthwise

Handful baby spinach leaves

4 cups chicken broth

1 large onion, chopped

1½ cups farro

8 slices English cucumber

DIRECTIONS

1 In a food processor, combine the almonds and half the garlic. Pulse a few times to coarsely chop. Add the arugula, lemon, Parmesan, and a few grinds of black pepper. Pulse again until the arugula is finely chopped. With the machine running, slowly drizzle in ½ cup olive oil. Continue to process until well blended. Taste, season with salt if needed, and set aside.

2 Trim a circle from the end of each olive. Cut each portion of bell pepper into 2 eyelids and a pair of lips, as shown.

3 In a small saucepan, warm the broth over low heat. Keep warm. In a heavy-bottom pot over medium heat, warm the remaining 2 tablespoons of olive oil. Add the onion and cook, stirring occasionally, until softened, about 3 minutes. Add the remaining 3 cloves garlic and cook until fragrant, 1 minute. Add the farro and cook, stirring frequently, until lightly toasted, about 2 minutes.

4 Add ¾ cup of the broth and cook, stirring frequently, until absorbed. Continue to add the broth, ½ cup at a time, stirring all the while and letting the broth absorb into the farro between each addition. Once the farro is nearly tender (after you've added about 3½ cups of broth), stir in pesto.

5 Add another ½ cup of broth and continue to stir. The farro should be creamy and tender at this point. Remove the risotto from the heat.

6 To assemble each serving, spoon a quarter of the risotto into a shallow bowl. Set two cucumber eyes dotted with olive pupils in place, as shown. Add a spinach-leaf crest, and bell pepper eyelids and a mouth. Repeat with the remaining risotto and toppings. Serve immediately.

Mickey's TACO CONES

PREP
5 min

COOK
30 min

SERVES
4

Give your favorite flour tortilla fixings a **MOUSE-EARS MAKEOVER!** We like the combo of ingredients here, but really, any you like will do. This recipe is as much about cooking as it is about the **FUN OF EATING** it once it's complete.

INGREDIENTS

5 (8-inch) flour tortillas

Cooking spray

1½ cups finely shredded cheddar

1 tablespoon vegetable oil

1 pound ground beef

1 recipe taco seasoning mix (see Dante's Blue Corn Tacos, page 138)

1 (16-ounce) can refried beans

3 cups shredded iceberg lettuce

½ cup guacamole

¼ cup sour cream

Additional taco toppings such as tomatoes, sliced black olives, diced onion, and salsa

TORTILLA CONE HOW-TO ↷

DIRECTIONS

1 Heat the oven to 400°F and line a baking sheet with parchment paper. With a 1½-inch round cookie cutter, shape 8 circles from a tortilla. Arrange them on the baking sheet, then spray both sides of each with cooking spray. Bake until golden, about 6 minutes.

2 Place a tortilla on a microwave-safe plate and sprinkle the edges with ¼ cup shredded cheddar, as shown. Place in the microwave and heat on high power for 30 seconds. While the cheese is melty, roll the tortilla into a cone, as shown. Stuff the center with parchment paper to help it hold its shape. Repeat with the remaining tortillas and cheese. Seal the end of each cone by adding a tablespoon of cheese to the tip. Microwave on high power for 30 seconds and press to seal. Set aside.

3 In a large skillet over medium heat, warm the vegetable oil. Add the beef and the seasoning mix, and cook until browned. In a small saucepan over low heat, combine the beans with 3 tablespoons water. Warm through.

4 To assemble each cone, remove the parchment, then stuff with ½ cup shredded lettuce. Top with beef and a scoop of refried beans. Add a dollop of guacamole and sour cream, then sprinkle with shredded cheese and other preferred toppings. Finish by adding two Mickey ears, as shown. Serve immediately.

Nemo's No Fish TACOS

PREP
10 min

COOK
50 min

SERVES
4

Tofu takes the place of fried fish in these **ALL-VEG TACOS**. Each faux fillet is coated in panko and oven baked to achieve the same tasty texture as the **CLASSIC** version, but with **LIGHTER** results.

INGREDIENTS

1 (14-ounce) package firm tofu

1 tablespoon finely chopped garlic

3 tablespoons olive oil

¼ teaspoon kosher salt

¼ teaspoon black pepper

1 cup panko bread crumbs

½ cup shredded green cabbage

½ cup shredded purple cabbage

¼ cup shredded carrots

1 lime, halved

1 bunch cilantro, finely chopped

½ cup plain Greek yogurt

1 teaspoon ground cumin

8 (6-inch) corn tortillas, warmed

4 black olives

Special equipment
Fish-shaped cookie cutter

DIRECTIONS

1. Heat the oven to 375°F. Evenly slice the tofu into 4 square slabs. Press each with a paper towel to remove excess water. Cut the tofu with the fish-shaped cookie cutter and place in a baking dish.

2. In a medium bowl, stir together the garlic, olive oil, and ⅛ teaspoon each of the salt and pepper. Pour the mixture over the tofu, making sure to coat all sides. Marinate at room temperature for 10 minutes.

3. Place the panko crumbs in a shallow dish. Evenly coat each tofu fish with the panko by pressing it into the crumbs on all sides. Arrange the tofu fillets on a baking sheet and bake until golden, flipping halfway through, about 30 minutes.

4. While the tofu bakes, make the slaw and sauce. Cut the lime into 4 wedges. In a medium bowl, toss together both cabbages, the carrot, the juice of one lime wedge, and the cilantro, salt, and pepper. In a small bowl, stir together the yogurt, cumin, and the juice of another lime wedge.

5. To assemble each taco, arrange a bed of slaw on a tortilla, then top with one or two tofu fish and a squeeze from the remaining lime wedges. Use the end of a straw to cut eyes from the olives, then add one to each fish. Use the yogurt sauce to drizzle on stripes. Serve immediately.

Dante's BLUE CORN TACOS

PREP
5 min

COOK
25 min

SERVES
8

Miguel's hairless, googly-eyed **DOG** is his guide and **PROTECTOR** throughout the worlds of the living and the dead. Dante's **PLAYFUL** canine face can also add a humorous twist to your regular **TACO** night.

INGREDIENTS

For the tacos

20 black olives

4 slices white cheddar

16 blue corn tortilla chips

8 blue corn taco shells

1 tablespoon canola oil

1 pound ground beef or turkey

½ cup shredded cheddar

1 cup diced tomatoes

1½ cups finely shredded red cabbage

Salsa or your favorite condiments for serving

For the seasoning mix

4 teaspoons chili powder

2 teaspoons ground cumin

1 teaspoon smoked paprika

½ teaspoon garlic powder

¾ teaspoon dried oregano

1 teaspoon salt

½ teaspoon black pepper

DIRECTIONS

1. Heat the oven to 350°F. Trim circles from the ends of 16 olives for the eyes and discard the scraps. Halve the remaining olives lengthwise for the noses. Use a mini round cutter to shape the cheese slices into 16 circles for the eyes. Trim 8 pieces from the scraps to adhere the noses. Break the tortilla chips into ear shapes, as shown.

2. Arrange the taco shells on a baking sheet. Set 2 cheddar-slice eyes and 2 olive pupils in place on each taco, as shown. Add a cheese scrap to each face and top with an olive nose. Place the shells in the oven until the cheese begins to melt, about 3 minutes.

3. In a small bowl, stir together all the ingredients for the seasoning mix. In a large skillet over medium-high heat, warm the oil. Add the ground beef or turkey and sprinkle on the seasoning mix. Cook until the meat is fully browned, about 6 minutes. Transfer to a paper towel–lined plate. To assemble each taco, fill a taco shell with ⅛ of the taco meat and top with cheddar, diced tomato, and shredded cabbage. Finish with a pair of tortilla-chip ears. Serve immediately with salsa or your favorite condiments.

Mulan's Blossom STIR-FRY

PREP
10 min

COOK
25 min

SERVES
3

Chopping veggies **UNIFORMLY** is an essential step in making a great stir-fry. We've taken things up a notch by adding a few fancy flower-shaped cuts as a subtle nod to **MULAN**. But don't fret! You won't need expert skills to pull them off—just a mini shape cutter and a **STEADY HAND**.

INGREDIENTS

1 large red bell pepper, trimmed and quartered lengthwise

1 large purple carrot, peeled

½ cup vegetable oil

7 ounces extra-firm tofu, pressed and cut into 1-inch cubes

½ cup soy sauce

¼ cup fresh-squeezed orange juice

5 teaspoons maple syrup

2 tablespoons sesame oil

2 teaspoons cornstarch

1-inch piece ginger, finely chopped

2 scallions, sliced

3 ounces shiitake mushrooms, sliced

6 ounces green beans, trimmed and halved

Cooked flat noodles, for serving

Special equipment
Mini flower cookie cutter

DIRECTIONS

1 Use a mini flower cookie cutter to cut the bell pepper pieces into blossom shapes. With a sharp knife, score 4 wide lines along the length of the carrot, as shown, then slice into flowers.

2 Line a plate with paper towels. In a large skillet over medium-high heat, warm the vegetable oil. Fry the tofu in batches until golden, about 3 minutes per side. Drain on the prepared plate.

3 In a small bowl, whisk together the soy sauce, orange juice, maple syrup, 1 tablespoon sesame oil, and the cornstarch until the cornstarch is dissolved.

4 In a large skillet or wok over medium-high heat, warm the remaining sesame oil. Add the ginger and scallions, and cook 1 minute. Add the bell pepper and cook, stirring constantly, 3 minutes. Stir in the mushrooms and green beans, add 2 tablespoons water, cover, and steam 3 minutes. Add the carrots and cook 1 minute, then add the prepared sauce and tofu. Let simmer undisturbed for 1 minute to let the sauce thicken. Stir to coat the vegetables completely with the sauce. Remove from heat and serve immediately over cooked noodles.

CARROT FLOWERS HOW-TO ➤

Mini (No Meat!) SHEPHERDESS PIES

PREP
15 min

COOK
1 hr 15 min

SERVES
6

Only the **INGENUITY** of Bo Peep could **COMPEL** us to try to make a classic meat pie with only veggies. We swapped in lentils for lamb, and the resulting dish, with a **BILLOWY** topping of potatoes and cauliflower, is every bit as good as the **ORIGINAL**.

INGREDIENTS

For the topping
3 large russet potatoes, cut into 1-inch cubes

½ head cauliflower, cut into florets

2 tablespoons unsalted butter

3 tablespoons grated Parmesan cheese

1½ teaspoons kosher salt

¼ teaspoon pepper

2 to 4 tablespoons whole milk

For the filling
1½ cups brown lentils

1 bay leaf, halved

1¾ cups vegetable broth

2 tablespoons olive oil

1 large onion, diced

1 medium carrot, peeled and diced

1 large stalk celery, diced

1 cup baby button mushrooms, halved

¼ cup dry red wine

1 teaspoon kosher salt

¼ teaspoon black pepper

2 tablespoons flour

1 tablespoon fresh chopped thyme

For the lamb faces
18 black olives

12 slices baguette

DIRECTIONS

1 Start the topping and cook the lentils. Place the potatoes and cauliflower in a basket and steam until tender, about 15 minutes. In a small pot, combine the lentils, bay leaf, 1 cup broth, and 3 cups water. Bring to a boil, then reduce the heat to a simmer and cook until the lentils are tender, about 20 minutes. Drain, discard the bay leaf, and set aside.

2 Transfer the potatoes and cauliflower to a food processor. Add the butter, Parmesan, salt, pepper, and 2 tablespoons milk. Blend until smooth. If needed, add 1 or 2 more tablespoons milk to achieve the desired consistency. Set aside.

3 In a large pan over medium heat, warm the olive oil. Add the onion, carrot, and celery, and cook until tender, about 5 minutes. Add the mushrooms and cook until they release their juices, about 3 minutes. Add the wine, salt, and pepper, and cook until the liquid is reduced by half. Stir in the flour, remaining ¾ cup broth, and thyme. Let cook until thickened slightly.

4 Heat the oven to 400°F. Evenly divide the filling among 6 small ramekins (we used 4-inch). Top each with ¾ cup of the potato mixture (reserve the remaining). Place the pies on a baking sheet and bake until the tops are puffed and the filling is bubbly, about 25 minutes.

5 While the pies cool slightly, trim the olives into 6 pairs of eyes and 6 noses. Halve 6 of the baguette slices for ears. Use the leftover potato topping to attach a face to each pie, as shown. Serve immediately.

Serpent's STEW

PREP
10 min

COOK
1 hr

SERVES
6

From Jafar to Juju, **SNAKES**—both good and evil—are recurrent characters in Disney films. Here they make a cameo as breadsticks that top a kale and white bean stew. **BEWARE** of the spicy bite from the chorizo!

INGREDIENTS

For the serpent breadsticks

¾ to 1 pound pizza dough

Flour, for dusting

1 tablespoon peppercorns

For the stew

2 tablespoons olive oil

1 (14-ounce) package chorizo, thinly sliced

1 large onion, chopped

3 garlic cloves, minced

1½ teaspoons kosher salt

¼ teaspoon black pepper

4 cups chicken broth

3 medium Yukon Gold potatoes, peeled and cut into 1-inch cubes

½ large bunch green kale, torn into bite-size pieces (about 6 cups)

1 (14-ounce) can white beans, rinsed and drained

DIRECTIONS

1 Heat the oven to 400°F and line two baking sheets with parchment paper. Divide the dough into 8 to 10 portions. On a lightly floured surface, roll a portion into a 2-foot-long rope. Working directly on one of the prepared sheets, wind and shape the rope into a serpent. Repeat with the remaining dough, spacing them 2 inches apart.

2 Press a pair of peppercorn eyes into each snake. Bake the snakes until golden and puffed, about 10 minutes. Set aside to cool.

3 In a large pot over medium heat, warm the oil. Add the chorizo and cook until browned, about 8 minutes. Transfer the meat to a bowl. Add the onion to the pan and cook until softened, about 3 minutes. Add the garlic and cook 1 minute. Season with the salt and pepper, then add the broth and 3 cups water, and bring to a boil.

4 Place the potatoes in the pot and reduce the heat to a simmer. Continue to simmer until the potatoes are cooked through, about 12 minutes. Remove half the stew from the pot and puree. Add it back to the pot along with the kale and white beans, and return to a simmer. Cook until the kale is wilted, about 8 minutes. Serve each portion hot in a bowl topped with a serpent breadstick.

BYO POTATO BAR

PREP
10 min

COOK
50 min

SERVES
4

As far as **DINNERTIME** options, a baked potato is as easy as it gets. But that doesn't mean your meal has to be boring! While the **POTATOES** are in the oven, prep bowls of toppings. (We suggest some below.) At the table, **EVERYONE** can use their **FAVORITES** to make a face before they dig in.

INGREDIENTS

For the potatoes
4 large russet potatoes

Olive oil

Butter

Kosher salt

Black pepper

Toppings
Sliced cheese, cut into small rounds

Sour cream

Cooked black beans

Cooked bacon

Corn kernels

Sliced olives

Chopped scallions

Baby bell peppers

DIRECTIONS

1 Heat the oven to 400°F. Set a rack over a baking sheet. Use the tines of a fork to pierce several holes in each potato, then coat each one with olive oil. Set on the rack.

2 Bake the potatoes until tender, about 45 minutes. Cut a slit in the top of each, use a fork to gently fluff the flesh, and season with butter, salt, and pepper. Serve hot and garnish with your favorite toppings.

Shredded cheese hair,
sour cream and black bean eyes,
baby carrot nose,
olive slice mouth

Shredded cheese hair,
olive eyes, rainbow carrot cheeks,
baby bell pepper nose and mouth

Bacon hair, olive slice eyes,
baby bell pepper nose
and mouth

Bacon hair, sour cream
and black bean eyes,
baby bell pepper mouth,
corn kernel teeth

Scallion hair, olive slice eyes,
carrot slice ears,
baby bell pepper nose
and mouth

Chapter

5

INSPIRED FEASTS

EVERY NOW AND AGAIN OUR DINNERTIME repertoire could use a little something new, and the recipes in this chapter were created with just that in mind. Some will be easy to fold right into your weeknight routine (see Hundred-Acre Wood Pasta, page 175), and others are better suited for the slower pace of the weekend (see the Ratatouille Trio recipes on page 166). But no matter which recipes you choose, we think you'll find at least a few here that you'll want to put on REPEAT.

Ham FRIED RICE

PREP
10 min

COOK
20 min

SERVES
4

This **HAWAIIAN-STYLE** version of pork fried rice is a **TASTY** introduction to a classic island-style dish. Even **BETTER**, you'll likely find most of the ingredients in your pantry or freezer.

INGREDIENTS

2 tablespoons vegetable oil

10 ounces canned ham, cut into ½-inch cubes

1 small onion, diced

2 cloves garlic, minced

2 teaspoons grated ginger

1 teaspoon sesame oil

1 large carrot, peeled and diced

¾ cup frozen corn, thawed

½ cup frozen peas, thawed

3 tablespoons soy sauce

2 eggs, lightly whisked

3 cups cooked white rice

¼ cup sliced green onions

DIRECTIONS

1 In a large, nonstick skillet over medium-high heat, warm 1 tablespoon vegetable oil. Add the ham and onion and cook until the meat is browned and slightly crisped on the edges, and the onions have softened, about 5 minutes. Add garlic and ginger and cook until fragrant, 1 minute.

2 Add the remaining vegetable oil, sesame oil, carrot, corn, peas, and soy sauce, and cook until the vegetables are tender, about 5 minutes. Push the mixture to the side, add the eggs, and scramble until cooked through, about 3 minutes. Add the rice and continue to cook until well blended and warmed through, about 2 minutes more. Serve immediately topped with green onions.

Lady and the Tramp Sheet Pan MEATBALLS and GRAVY

PREP
5 min

COOK
35 min

SERVES
6

Making your own meatballs and red sauce may seem like a daunting task, but we've STREAMLINED the process without sacrificing the FLAVOR. Serve this duo with a side of toasted bread, or pair it with a plate of SPAGHETTI just like Lady and Tramp.

INGREDIENTS

For the red sauce

1 tablespoon olive oil

1 large onion, chopped

3 cloves garlic, minced

2 (28-ounce) cans diced tomatoes

1 bay leaf

6 sprigs fresh thyme or oregano

1 teaspoon kosher salt

½ teaspoon black pepper

1 tablespoon butter

For the meatballs

½ pound ground beef

½ pound ground pork

½ cup panko bread crumbs

¼ cup grated Parmesan

2 eggs

2 teaspoons chopped fresh oregano

1 tablespoon chopped fresh parsley

¼ cup finely chopped shallots

DIRECTIONS

1 In a large skillet over medium heat, warm the oil. Add the onion and cook until softened, about 4 minutes. Add the garlic and cook 1 minute. Add the tomatoes, bay leaf, fresh herbs, salt, and pepper, and stir to combine.

2 Bring the sauce to a boil, then reduce the heat and let simmer 10 minutes. Remove from the heat and pluck out the herb stems and bay leaf.

3 Place half the sauce in a blender and puree. Add the puree back to the pan, place over low heat, and stir in the butter. Remove from the heat, cover, and set aside.

4 Line a baking sheet with foil and set the broiler to high with a rack 6 inches away from the heat. In a large bowl, use your hands to combine the meatball ingredients and toss until evenly blended. Do not overmix.

5 Scoop a golf-ball-size portion of the meatball mixture and shape it into a ball. Transfer to the prepared baking sheet. Continue with remaining mixture, spacing the meatballs ½ inch apart.

6 Broil the meatballs for 4 minutes, then remove from the oven, flip, and broil 4 minutes more. Serve immediately with pasta sauce and, if you like, your favorite pasta.

Incredibles Superfood SALMON BOWL

PREP
15 min

COOK
15 min

SERVES
2

We can't offer a recipe that will give you the Parrs' **SUPERNATURAL** abilities, but we do have this alternative: a savory grain bowl that's packed with superfood bona fides like brown rice, edamame, and salmon. Think of it as a **WHOLESOME** meal for the superhero-adjacent.

INGREDIENTS

For the orange-miso dressing

2 tablespoons miso

6 tablespoons canola oil

1 small garlic clove, grated

1 teaspoon grated ginger

¼ cup fresh-squeezed orange juice

1 tablespoon honey

Splash rice wine vinegar

For the bowl

3 tablespoons butter, room temperature

2 teaspoons red miso

1 scallion, minced, white and light green parts only

2 (4- to 5-ounce) salmon fillets

2 cups cooked brown rice

2 cups kale chips (see Arlo's Kale Chips, page 54)

1 cup frozen shelled edamame, thawed

1 small carrot, cut into matchsticks

2 Persian cucumbers, sliced

2 tablespoons chopped cilantro

DIRECTIONS

1 In a small bowl, whisk together all the ingredients for the dressing. Cover and refrigerate until ready to use.

2 Heat the oven to 425°F and line a small baking sheet with foil. In a small bowl, mash together the butter, miso, and scallion. Arrange the salmon fillets on the pan and spread each fillet with half the butter. Bake until cooked through, about 10 minutes.

3 To assemble, evenly divide the rice between two bowls. Top each with a salmon fillet, and half the vegetables. Garnish with cilantro and serve immediately.

Mamá Coco's EMPANADAS

PREP
5 min

COOK
1 hr

MAKES
15

Paired with a **SALAD OR SLAW**, these **HANDHELD** meat pies make a light and tasty work lunch. Make a **BIG BATCH** and freeze them ahead of time for a real grab-and-go option you can toss right into your bag.

INGREDIENTS

1 tablespoon canola oil

1 large onion, diced

½ large red bell pepper, chopped

1 clove garlic, minced

¾ teaspoon chili powder

⅛ teaspoon cayenne pepper

4 teaspoons ground cumin

¾ teaspoon kosher salt

1 pound ground beef

2 tablespoons tomato paste

¼ cup chopped green olives

¼ to ½ cup chicken broth

15 empanada wrappers, thawed

1 egg

DIRECTIONS

1 In a large skillet over medium heat, warm the oil. Add the onion and bell pepper and cook, stirring occasionally, until softened, about 5 minutes. Add the garlic, chili powder, cayenne, cumin, and salt, and cook until fragrant, about 1 minute. Add the beef and cook, stirring occasionally, until beginning to brown, about 5 minutes.

2 Stir in the tomato paste, green olives, and ¼ cup chicken broth. Simmer, stirring occasionally, 10 minutes, to let the flavors meld. If needed, add more broth 1 tablespoon at a time as it cooks. (The mixture should be moist, but not watery.) Remove from heat and let cool.

3 Heat the oven to 400°F and line two baking sheets with parchment paper. Place an empanada wrapper on your work surface and spoon 2 tablespoons of the beef mixture onto one half. Fold the other half of the wrapper over the filling and press gently to seal. Fold in the corners of the empanada, then crimp by folding the top edge over itself. (Alternately, crimp the edge with a fork.) Place the empanada on a baking sheet and repeat with the remaining wrappers and filling, spacing them evenly on the pans.

4 In a small bowl, whisk together the egg with 1 tablespoon water. Brush the tops of the empanadas with the egg wash. Bake until golden and warmed through, about 18 minutes.

Kalua PORK SLIDERS

PREP
5 min

COOK
4 hr 10 min
(includes slow cooking)

MAKES
6 to 8

TRADITIONALLY, Kalua-style pork is made in an imu, a Hawaiian underground oven made with wood and stones. For this version, liquid smoke gives the meat FLAVOR like it was pulled straight from the fire while slow cooking ensures it's moist and tender. Place it on a bun and top with CARAMELIZED pineapple for a delicious, island-inspired bite.

INGREDIENTS

3-pound Boston pork butt shoulder roast

2 tablespoons liquid smoke

1 tablespoon Hawaiian pink salt

3 to 4 small pineapple slices

1 tablespoon canola oil

6 to 8 slider buns

Sriracha sauce, for serving

DIRECTIONS

1 Use a fork to pierce the roast on all sides. Rub the roast with the liquid smoke and salt. Place in a slow cooker and cook on high 4 hours, until the roast is tender and beginning to fall apart. Remove from the slow cooker along with the juices and shred with two forks. Keep warm.

2 Brush the pineapple on both sides with the oil and arrange on the baking sheet. Broil on high until slightly charred, about 3 minutes per side. Keep close watch as they broil so they don't burn. Halve each slice and set aside.

3 To assemble each slider, spoon pork onto a bottom bun. Top with pineapple and cover with the top bun. Repeat with the remaining pork, buns, and pineapple. Serve immediately with sriracha sauce.

Tow Mater's Balsamic CHICKEN LEGS

PREP
5 min

COOK
45 min

SERVES
4

Take a **BREAK** from on-the road eats and try these chicken drumsticks **DOUSED** in a **HOMEMADE** herby balsamic glaze. While they finish in the oven, you can throw **TOGETHER** a simple side like Aladdin's Fattoush Salad on page 94.

INGREDIENTS

1 cup balsamic vinegar

¼ cup honey

2 sprigs fresh rosemary

1 teaspoon orange zest

1 tablespoon fresh orange juice

Kosher salt

8 chicken drumsticks

Black pepper

1 tablespoon olive oil

DIRECTIONS

1 Heat the oven to 425°F. In a medium skillet over medium heat, combine the vinegar, honey, and rosemary. Cook, stirring frequently, until thickened and reduced, about 15 minutes. Remove from the heat, stir in the orange zest and juice, and season with salt. Set aside.

2 Pat the chicken dry with paper towels and season with salt and pepper. Heat the oil in a large skillet. Working in batches if needed, brown the chicken legs on each side until golden and crisp, about 3 minutes per side. Transfer to a large baking dish.

3 Reserve a few tablespoons of the glaze for serving, then use the rest to brush the chicken on all sides with the sauce. Place in the oven and bake 10 minutes. Remove from the oven, baste once more, then continue to bake until cooked through, about 10 minutes. Place under the broiler to char slightly, about 2 minutes. Brush with the reserved sauce and serve immediately.

Kronk's SPINACH PUFFS

PREP
5 min

COOK
35 min

MAKES
18

GROOVE into something **SAVORY** instead of sweet! These **IMPRESSIVE** little bundles of spinach and cheese are baked in a pan and bring together the flavors of **SPANAKOPITA** without the fuss of phyllo dough.

INGREDIENTS

1 pound frozen spinach, thawed

4 scallions, chopped

$\frac{1}{3}$ cup crumbled feta

$\frac{1}{3}$ cup cottage cheese

2 tablespoons shredded Parmesan

3 eggs

$\frac{3}{4}$ teaspoon kosher salt

$\frac{1}{8}$ teaspoon white pepper

2 sheets frozen puff pastry from a 17-ounce package, thawed

DIRECTIONS

1 Heat the oven to 400°F. Use a mesh colander or cheesecloth to squeeze and drain the water from the spinach. Place in a medium bowl with the scallions, feta, cottage cheese, Parmesan, 2 eggs, and the salt and pepper. Stir to combine.

2 Evenly cut each pastry sheet into 9 squares. Press each dough portion into the well of a standard cupcake pan, letting the corners hang over the edges. Spoon a generous tablespoon of the spinach mixture into each pastry.

3 Gather the corners of each dough square and pinch them closed. In a small bowl, whisk together the remaining egg with 1 tablespoon water. Brush the tops of the pastries with egg wash, then bake until golden and crisp, about 25 minutes. Let cool slightly before serving.

Ratatouille Casserole (page 168)

RATATOUILLE
Trio

The VEGETABLES in each of these dishes may be the same, but switching up the cooking techniques and a few ingredients makes each one UNIQUE—a small bit of culinary ingenuity that might even impress CHEF REMY. We suggest trying all three to see which you like best (though not necessarily at the same time!). No matter which you decide to cook, they're equally delicious served with a BAGUETTE or a side of rice.

Sheet Pan Ratatouille with Smoked Sausage (page 168)

Remy's Ratatouille with Poached Eggs (page 169)

SHEET PAN RATATOUILLE with Smoked Sausage

PREP: 10 min • COOK: 35 min • SERVES: 4

INGREDIENTS

¼ cup chopped basil

1 medium zucchini, sliced into ½-inch-thick semicircles

1 medium yellow squash, sliced into ½-inch-thick semicircles

1 small eggplant, cut into 1-inch cubes

4 smoked pork sausages, sliced into thirds

¾ teaspoon smoked paprika

1 cup cherry tomatoes, halved

6 baby bell peppers, trimmed and quartered

2 tablespoons olive oil

½ teaspoon kosher salt

1 teaspoon herbes de Provence

DIRECTIONS

1 Heat the oven to 425°F. Line two baking sheets with parchment paper.

2 Toss half the basil and the remaining ingredients in a large bowl. Distribute evenly among the baking sheets. Do not crowd the pans. Roast, stirring once, until the vegetables begin to caramelize and char slightly, about 25 minutes. Serve immediately topped with the remaining basil.

RATATOUILLE CASSEROLE

PREP: 5 min • COOK: 1 hr 5 min • SERVES: 8

INGREDIENTS

2 tablespoons olive oil

1 large onion, diced

1 medium green bell pepper, diced

2 garlic cloves, minced

¾ teaspoon kosher salt

¼ teaspoon black pepper

1 (28-ounce) can diced tomatoes

7 sprigs fresh thyme

4 basil leaves

3 medium zucchini

3 medium yellow squash

2 Chinese eggplant

5 slender Roma tomatoes

½ teaspoon herbes de Provence

DIRECTIONS

1 In a large pan over medium heat, warm 1 tablespoon olive oil. Add the onion and bell pepper and cook until softened, about 5 minutes. Add the garlic, ½ teaspoon salt, and the peppers and cook 1 minute. Stir in the diced tomatoes, 4 sprigs thyme, and the basil leaves. Bring to a simmer and cook until thickened, about 15 minutes.

2 As the sauce simmers, slice the zucchini, yellow squash, eggplant, and Roma tomatoes into ⅛-inch-thick rounds. Heat the oven to 400°F.

3 Transfer the tomato sauce to a heat-safe bowl and remove any stems. Use an immersion blender to puree it until smooth. Spoon enough sauce to cover the bottom of a deep-dish pie plate by ½ inch (and reserve the rest for topping the ratatouille, or use in another dish).

4 Stack the sliced vegetables in alternating order, then arrange them in concentric circles inside the pan. Drizzle with the remaining tablespoon olive oil and sprinkle with the

remaining ¼ teaspoon salt. Break the remaining sprigs of thyme into pieces and scatter over the top, along with the herbes de Provence. Cover the casserole with foil and bake 30 minutes. Remove the foil and bake until the vegetables are completely tender, about 15 minutes more. Let cool slightly before serving with additional sauce.

REMY'S RATATOUILLE with Poached Eggs

PREP: 5 min • COOK: 35 min • SERVES: 4

INGREDIENTS

2 tablespoons olive oil

1 red onion, sliced

4 garlic cloves, minced

1 small eggplant, cut into ½-inch cubes

1 medium zucchini, cut into ½-inch cubes

1 medium yellow squash, cut into ½-inch cubes

1 large red bell pepper, diced

4 sprigs thyme

¼ teaspoon kosher salt

¼ teaspoon black pepper

1 (28-ounce) can crushed tomatoes

4 eggs

DIRECTIONS

1 Heat the oven to 375°F. In a large oven-safe skillet over medium heat, warm the oil. Add the onion and cook until softened, about 5 minutes. Add the garlic and cook 1 minute.

2 Stir in the eggplant, zucchini, yellow squash, bell pepper, thyme, salt, and pepper. Sauté, stirring occasionally, until the vegetables begin to soften, about 6 minutes. Add the crushed tomatoes, cover, and cook, stirring occasionally, until the vegetables are completely tender, about 10 minutes.

3 Use a spoon to make 4 wells in the ratatouille. Crack an egg into each well and place the skillet in the oven. Bake until the whites of the eggs are set, about 8 minutes. Serve immediately.

Pooh's Honey-Roasted Veggie GRAIN BOWL

PREP
5 min

COOK
35 min

SERVES
2

POOH would likely prefer his vegetables slathered just in **HONEY**, but we know your tastes are more refined. The sauce for this grain bowl—a **LIGHTLY SWEET** and earthy blend of honey, turmeric, and Dijon mustard—is used for both basting the vegetables before they're cooked and **DRIZZLING** when they're ready to serve. It's a nourishing way to satisfy a "rumbly tumbly."

INGREDIENTS

For the dressing

2 tablespoons honey

1 tablespoon Dijon mustard

1 tablespoon apple cider vinegar

1 garlic clove, minced

½ teaspoon ground turmeric

½ teaspoon kosher salt

⅛ teaspoon black pepper

⅓ cup olive oil

For the vegetables

2 large carrots, peeled, halved, and cut into 2-inch lengths

1 medium sweet potato, peeled and cut into 2-inch chunks

4 baby zucchini, halved lengthwise

6 yellow baby bell peppers, quartered

2 cups cooked brown rice, for serving

Handful grape tomatoes, halved

¼ cup canned chickpeas, rinsed and drained

Toasted sesame seeds, for garnish

DIRECTIONS

1 Heat the oven to 400°F and line a baking sheet with parchment paper. In a small bowl, whisk together the honey, Dijon mustard, apple cider vinegar, garlic, turmeric, salt, and pepper. Whisk in the olive oil in a slow, steady stream to emulsify.

2 In a small bowl, combine the carrots and sweet potato with 1 tablespoon of the dressing (reserve the bowl for tossing the remaining vegetables). Transfer to a baking sheet and roast 15 minutes. Place the zucchini and bell peppers in the bowl and toss with 2 teaspoons of the dressing. Add them to the roasting pan and roast all the vegetables until beginning to brown in spots, about 10 minutes.

3 Divide the rice between two bowls. Top each with half the roasted vegetables, along with half the tomatoes and chickpeas. Serve immediately with extra dressing and sesame seeds on the side.

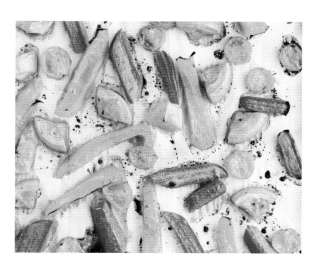

Conch Shell
MAC and CHEESE

PREP
5 min

COOK
50 min

SERVES
6 to 8

The **SECRET** to a creamy mac and cheese starts with the sauce—in this case a basic béchamel made by heating and whisking together flour, butter, and milk until rich and **VELVETY**. Blended with a trio of cheeses and an **UNEXPECTED** shell-shaped pasta, it's islands away from the boxed stuff.

INGREDIENTS

¾ pound medium pasta shells

2 teaspoons kosher salt, plus more for boiling the pasta

5 tablespoons butter, plus more for greasing the pan

5 tablespoons flour

2½ cups whole milk

2 cups shredded sharp cheddar

1 cup shredded Gruyère

⅓ cup shredded Parmesan

3 tablespoons panko bread crumbs, lightly toasted

DIRECTIONS

1 Heat the oven to 350°F. Bring a large pot of water to a boil. Season generously with salt, then add the pasta and cook until al dente, according to the package directions.

2 Grease an 8-inch baking dish with butter. In a high-sided heavy-bottom pan over medium-low heat, melt the butter. Whisk in the flour until smooth. Whisking continuously, slowly pour in the milk, a little at a time. Continue to whisk until the mixture is smooth and has thickened slightly, about 3 minutes. Remove from the heat. Stir in the salt.

3 In a large bowl, combine the pasta and roux. Stir to coat evenly. Add the cheese and blend evenly once more. Pour the mixture into the prepared baking dish. Scatter the panko over the pasta. Bake until bubbly and the topping is golden brown, about 30 minutes.

Ingredient
SWAP

We prefer the flavor of sharp cheddar in our mac, but if you like more subtle flavors, you can also use mild cheddar.

Hundred-Acre Wood PASTA

PREP
5 min

COOK
30 min

SERVES
6

It's no **COINCIDENCE** that this forest-inspired, one-pot pasta is **FILLED** with trunks and trees—or more accurately, penne pasta and bite-size florets of broccoli and cauliflower. Lemon zest and fresh dill add the **BRIGHTNESS** of a little bear we know.

INGREDIENTS

3 slices stale whole grain bread

2 tablespoons olive oil

¾ pound penne pasta

1 teaspoon lemon zest, plus the juice of ½ a lemon

2 teaspoons kosher salt

½ teaspoon black pepper

2 cups broccoli florets

2 cups cauliflower florets

2 tablespoons chopped fresh dill, plus more for garnish

6 ounces goat cheese

DIRECTIONS

1. Heat the oven to 425°F. Tear the bread into bite-size pieces. On a baking sheet, toss with the olive oil, then spread evenly on the pan. Bake until golden and crisp, about 8 minutes.

2. In a large skillet, combine the pasta, lemon zest and juice, salt, and pepper with 4½ cups water. Bring to a boil, then reduce to a simmer and let cook 5 minutes. Add the broccoli and cauliflower and cook, stirring occasionally, until the pasta is tender, about 5 minutes more.

3. Stir in the dill and goat cheese. Toss until well coated. Season with more salt and pepper if desired. Transfer to a large bowl. Top with bread crumbs and, if you like, more dill before serving immediately.

Mowgli's MATAR PANEER

PREP
5 min

COOK
35 min

SERVES
4

A blend of warm, **AROMATIC** spices makes the rich tomato sauce in this recipe **COMFORTING** and delicious. It's even easy enough to make on a busy weeknight.

INGREDIENTS

2 tablespoons canola oil

1 large onion, chopped

3 garlic cloves, grated

1-inch piece fresh ginger, grated

1 (28-ounce) can diced tomatoes

½ teaspoon kosher salt

2 teaspoons cumin seeds

¾ teaspoon garam masala

¾ teaspoon ground turmeric

1 bay leaf

¼ teaspoon ground coriander

1 (8-ounce) package paneer, cut into 1-inch cubes

1¾ cups frozen peas

2 tablespoons heavy cream

2 cups cooked basmati rice, for serving

Fresh cilantro sprigs, for garnish

DIRECTIONS

1 In a large skillet over medium heat, warm 1 tablespoon canola oil. Add the onion and cook until softened, about 5 minutes. Add the garlic and ginger and cook 1 minute. Stir in the tomatoes and salt, then simmer for 10 minutes to let the flavors meld.

2 Transfer the sauce to a bowl and use an immersion blender to puree until smooth. Set aside.

3 Wipe the skillet clean and warm the remaining oil over medium heat. Add the cumin seeds, garam masala, turmeric, bay leaf, and coriander. Toast until fragrant, about 2 minutes. Return the sauce to the pan (carefully, as sauce may splatter a bit) and stir in ¾ cup water. Stir in the paneer and peas. Simmer, partially covered, stirring occasionally, until thickened, about 10 minutes. Stir in the heavy cream. Serve immediately over rice. Garnish with cilantro.

Roasted Broccoli
Pizza (page 180)

Pizza Planet DUO

These two pies—one with VEG, the other with MEAT—are
inspired by one of Andy's FAVORITE restaurants in the
Toy Story films. To save time, we suggest starting with
a store-bought dough. But if you've got the time (and a
favorite recipe), a HOMEMADE crust will make either of these
UNCONVENTIONAL pizzas even more irresistible.

Sausage Kale Pizza (page 181)

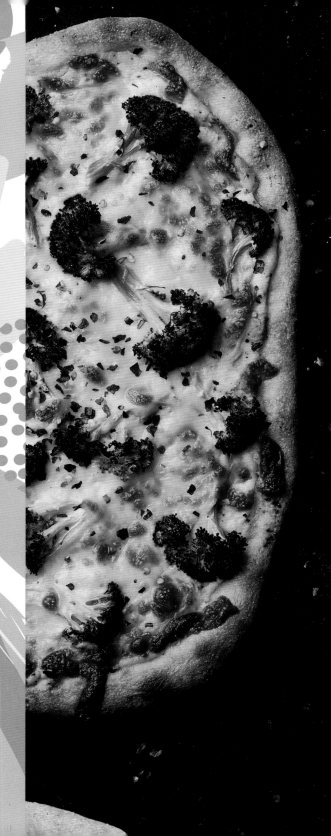

ROASTED BROCCOLI
Pizza

PREP: 5 min • COOK: 30 min • SERVES: 4

INGREDIENTS

1 large crown broccoli (about 4 cups) cut into florets

3 tablespoons olive oil

½ teaspoon kosher salt

¼ teaspoon black pepper

1 cup ricotta

2 cloves garlic, grated

Cornmeal for dusting

1 pound pizza dough, at room temperature

1½ cups grated fresh mozzarella

Red pepper flakes, for serving (optional)

DIRECTIONS

1 Heat the oven to 450°F. On a baking sheet, toss the broccoli with 4 teaspoons olive oil and season with ¼ teaspoon salt and ⅛ teaspoon pepper. Spread evenly on the sheet and bake until crisp tender, about 10 minutes. Increase the oven temperature to 500°F.

2 Meanwhile, in a small bowl, combine the ricotta, garlic, and remaining ¼ teaspoon salt and ⅛ teaspoon pepper.

3 Sprinkle a baking sheet with cornmeal. Press the pizza dough out into a large oval and transfer to the sheet. Top with the ricotta mixture, mozzarella, and roasted broccoli. Brush the edges of the pizza with the remaining olive oil.

4 Bake the pizza until the cheese has browned slightly and the edges are golden and crisp, about 15 minutes. Serve immediately, topped with red pepper flakes if using.

SAUSAGE KALE
Pizza

PREP: 5 min • COOK: 30 min • SERVES: 4

INGREDIENTS

1 tablespoon plus 2 teaspoons olive oil

6 ounces (about 2 small links) sweet Italian sausage

1½ cups green kale, torn into bite-size pieces

Cornmeal for dusting

1 pound pizza dough, at room temperature

1 cup of your favorite red pizza sauce

1½ cups shredded mozzarella

1 roasted red pepper, sliced

Grated Parmesan, for serving (optional)

DIRECTIONS

1 Heat the oven to 500°F. In a small pan over medium heat, warm 2 teaspoons olive oil. Add the sausage and cook, stirring occasionally and breaking it into pieces, until no longer pink, about 5 minutes. Drain on a paper towel–lined plate. In a medium bowl, toss together 1 teaspoon olive oil with the kale until coated.

2 Sprinkle a baking sheet with cornmeal. Press the dough and transfer to the baking sheet. Top with the sauce, then half each of the mozzarella, sausage, kale, and red bell pepper. Repeat the topping layers on the pizza. Brush the edges of the pizza with the remaining olive oil.

3 Bake the pizza until the cheese has browned slightly and the edges are golden and crisp, about 15 minutes. Serve immediately, topped with grated Parmesan, if using.

Geppetto's CACIO E PEPE

PREP
5 min

COOK
25 min

SERVES
6

Some of the **TASTIEST** dishes call for only a few ingredients, like this homey Italian classic we **IMAGINE** as a go-to dinner for the humble carpenter Geppetto. Serve with roasted veggies for a **COMPLETE** meal.

INGREDIENTS

Kosher salt

¾ pound spaghetti

2 tablespoons olive oil

3 tablespoons butter

2½ teaspoons black pepper

½ cup grated Parmesan

¾ cup grated Pecorino Romano

DIRECTIONS

1 Bring a pot of salted water to a boil. Cook the pasta according to the package directions, until al dente. Drain, reserving 1½ cups pasta water.

2 Combine the olive oil and butter in a large skillet over medium heat. Add the pepper and cook 1 minute. Stir in the pasta, along with ¾ cup pasta water. Remove from the heat, let cool 5 minutes, then gradually add half the cheese. Toss with tongs to coat the pasta. Add another ½ cup pasta water and the remaining cheese. Continue to toss until the pasta is evenly coated. If needed, add a few tablespoons pasta water to keep the pasta from becoming clumpy. Season with more salt and pepper if desired, then serve immediately.

Aunt Cass's WINGS

PREP
5 min

COOK
40 min

SERVES
8

If you don't believe you can make a good chicken wing by **OVEN ROASTING**, then we urge you to give this recipe a try. They won't crisp up like fried wings, but the high cooking temperature ensures that they'll be just as **TASTY** as any pub version—especially after they're brushed with **HOMEMADE** honey glaze.

INGREDIENTS

For the wings

1 tablespoon kosher salt

2 tablespoons paprika

2 tablespoons sugar

½ teaspoon black pepper

½ teaspoon ground turmeric

½ teaspoon ground cinnamon

¼ teaspoon cayenne pepper

⅛ teaspoon garlic powder

4 tablespoons canola or vegetable oil

4 pounds chicken wings, split with tips removed

For the sauce

1 tablespoon chili powder

½ teaspoon ground ginger

1 tablespoon ground coriander

2 tablespoons lime juice

½ cup soy sauce

1 cup honey

2 tablespoons cornstarch

DIRECTIONS

1 Heat the oven to 500°F. Line two baking sheets with foil. In a large bowl, stir together all the spices for the wings. Whisk in the oil, then add the wings and toss to coat.

2 Evenly divide the wings among the baking sheets and spread into an even layer. Bake until brown and charred in spots, about 35 minutes.

3 Meanwhile, in a medium saucepan over medium heat, combine the chili powder, ginger, coriander, lime juice, soy sauce, and honey with ½ cup water. Cook until warmed through, about 5 minutes. In a small bowl, combine the cornstarch with ¼ cup water. Whisk the mixture into the sauce and continue to cook, stirring constantly, until thickened. Remove from heat.

4 Brush the wings with the sauce and serve immediately.

One-Pan PASTA with TUNA

PREP
5 min

COOK
20 min

SERVES
4

This **SIMPLE** pasta dish is made for sharing just like the spaghetti and meatballs in *LADY AND THE TRAMP*. The recipe calls for tuna packed in oil, and we'd like to note that using higher-quality fish is well worth the **SPLURGE**.

INGREDIENTS

4 slices stale whole grain bread

3 tablespoons olive oil

¾ cup pitted Castelvetrano olives, torn

2 teaspoons lemon zest, plus juice of ½ a lemon

3 tablespoons chopped fresh dill, plus more for garnish

¾ pound spaghetti

1 teaspoon kosher salt

½ teaspoon black pepper

1 (7-ounce) jar tuna in olive oil, drained

DIRECTIONS

1 Heat the oven to 425°F. Tear the bread into bite-size pieces. On a baking sheet, toss with 1 tablespoon olive oil, then spread evenly on the pan. Bake until golden and crisp, about 8 minutes.

2 Combine the olives, lemon zest, dill, spaghetti, salt, pepper, and 4¼ cups water in a deep 10-inch skillet. Bring to a boil.

3 Reduce the heat to medium and continue to cook, stirring occasionally, until the water is mostly absorbed and the pasta is cooked through, about 8 minutes. (If the pasta becomes too dry before it's cooked through, add more water a few tablespoons at a time.) Add the tuna and remaining olive oil and toss until warmed through. Top with bread crumbs and, if you like, more dill before serving.

INSPIRED FEASTS 191

Chapter

6

Bayou ANDOUILLE and COLLARDS

PREP 5 min

COOK 40 min

SERVES 6

Two **ESSENTIAL** Southern ingredients are the centerpiece of this brothy stew that features tomatoes and a **GENEROUS** helping of smoke and spice thanks to the addition of **PAPRIKA**. While the cooking time will likely be adequate, be sure to test the collards before you take them off the heat. Larger leaves often require more **COOKING** time to become tender.

INGREDIENTS

1 cup farro

1 to 2 tablespoons olive oil

4 links andouille sausage, sliced

1 large onion, chopped

½ teaspoon smoked paprika

Kosher salt

Black pepper

2 cloves garlic, minced

1 (28-ounce) can whole tomatoes

2 small bunches collard greens, chopped (about 8 cups)

½ cup chicken broth

DIRECTIONS

1 Cook the farro according to the package directions. Meanwhile, in a large, heavy pot over medium heat, warm 1 tablespoon oil. Add the sausage and cook until browned, about 5 minutes. Transfer to a plate and reserve the rendered fat in the pan. If needed, add the remaining tablespoon of olive oil to coat the bottom of the pot.

2 Add the onion and cook, stirring occasionally, until softened, about 5 minutes. Add the paprika, season with salt and pepper, then add the garlic and cook until fragrant, about 1 minute. Working over the pot, use your hands to crush the tomatoes into bite-size pieces and add their juices. Use a wooden spoon to scrape the fond and brown bits from the bottom of the pot.

3 Add the collards and chicken broth. Stir until the collards are wilted, then cover tightly, reduce the heat to low, and simmer, stirring occasionally, for 20 minutes. Return the sausage to the pot, cover, and continue cooking until the collards are silky and tender, about 15 minutes more. Serve immediately over the farro.

Royal ROAST CHICKEN

PREP
10 min

COOK
About 1 hr

SERVES
8

After just one bite of this **FLAVORFUL** oven-baked chicken, even the most discerning tasters in your dining court will declare it **WORTHY** of making again. Seasoned with rosemary, fennel, and fresh lemon, this bird is fit for a **SPECIAL** feast with guests, but **HANDS-FREE** enough to be a winner any night of the week.

INGREDIENTS

5 tablespoons olive oil

1 large fennel bulb, trimmed and sliced lengthwise into ¼-inch-thick pieces, fronds reserved for garnish

4 cups baby red potatoes, halved

1 tablespoon plus ½ teaspoon kosher salt

¾ teaspoon black pepper

1 (3- to 4-pound) whole chicken

3 tablespoons chopped rosemary, plus more for garnish

1 lemon, sliced into wedges, plus more for serving

4 cloves garlic, smashed

DIRECTIONS

1 Heat the oven to 425°F. In a baking dish, combine 2 tablespoons olive oil with the fennel and baby potatoes. Spread evenly in the pan and season with ½ teaspoon salt and ¼ teaspoon pepper. Place the chicken directly on top of the vegetables. Drizzle with the remaining 3 tablespoons olive oil and remaining tablespoon salt, ¼ teaspoon pepper, and chopped rosemary.

2 Tuck the lemon wedges and garlic around the chicken, then bake until the skin is golden and crisp, and a thermometer inserted into a thigh reads 165°F, about 45 minutes to 1 hour. Carve and serve immediately with fresh lemon wedges. If you like, serve the bird on a platter garnished with fennel fronds and fresh rosemary, as shown.

Helpful TIP

Feel free to tinker with the fresh herbs in this recipe and add your favorites. Rosemary, thyme, and oregano—or even a combination of them—work best.

EVERYTHING for the HOLIDAYS

FEW HOLIDAYS ARE COMPLETE WITHOUT FAMILY, FRIENDS, AND OF COURSE, FOOD.

The recipes here have the potential to bring together all three by blending character-inspired bites you can indulge in on January 1 (see Fireworks over Magic Kingdom Cupcakes, page 194), December 25 (see Gingerbread Five Ways, page 224), and a host of dates in between.

Fireworks over Magic Kingdom CUPCAKES

PREP
5 min

COOK
30 min

MAKES
12

Toast to the New Year with a **SWEET** batch of cupcakes that mimic the **SHIMMERING** night sky at Magic Kingdom, and all over the world once the clock strikes midnight. The bursts of color are constructed by piping and layering **MELTING CHOCOLATE**—a decorating trick even a beginning baker will be able to pull off.

INGREDIENTS

½ cup orange candy melts

½ cup purple candy melts

½ cup yellow candy melts

1 cup vanilla frosting

Blue food coloring

Black food coloring

12 unfrosted chocolate cupcakes

1 tablespoon mini silver star sprinkles

1 tablespoon silver sanding sugar

DIRECTIONS

1 Line a baking sheet with parchment paper. Place each portion of candy melts in a heat-safe bowl and melt according to the package directions. Transfer each to a piping bag fit with a writing tip. Use the melted candy to pipe several firework bursts of different sizes onto the parchment. Layer shapes as desired. Let the candy set.

2 Place the frosting in a small bowl and tint it with a few drops of blue and a drop of black food coloring. Working with one cupcake at a time, cover the top with frosting, then scatter lightly with star sprinkles and sanding sugar. Finish with a few candy fireworks.

Lunar New Year VEGGIE DUMPLINGS

PREP
10 min

COOK
35 min

MAKES
About 24

In China, many **FAMILIES** gather on the eve of the new year to make and eat dumplings, which are said to represent wealth and **GOOD FORTUNE**. Rally your own crew to fold, then **FEAST** on this version for a deliciously memorable day.

INGREDIENTS

5 tablespoons vegetable oil

1-inch piece grated ginger

2 small garlic cloves, minced

1 cup chopped shiitake mushrooms

1 tablespoon sesame oil

2 cups Napa cabbage

¾ cup shredded carrot

⅓ cup chopped scallions

1 tablespoon soy sauce, plus more for serving

24 round dumpling wrappers

CRIMP DUMPLING HOW-TO

DIRECTIONS

1 In a large skillet over medium-high heat, warm 1 tablespoon vegetable oil. Add the ginger and garlic and cook until fragrant, about 1 minute. Add the mushrooms and cook until tender and most of the water has evaporated from the pan, about 5 minutes. Add the sesame oil, cabbage, carrot, scallions, and soy sauce, and cook until all the vegetables are wilted.

2 To make each dumpling, spoon a tablespoon of filling into the center of a wrapper. Dab the edges with water, fold in half, then crimp the dumpling and press to adhere each fold, as shown.

3 In a large, nonstick skillet over medium heat, warm a tablespoon of the remaining vegetable oil. Place several dumplings in the pan and cook until browned, about 3 minutes. Add 3 tablespoons water to the pan, then cover and steam until the dumplings are cooked through, about 3 minutes. Transfer to a plate, and repeat steps with the remaining dumplings, adding more oil to the pan as needed. Serve immediately with soy sauce.

Conversation Mouse COOKIES

PREP
5 min

COOK
3 hr
*(includes chilling
and setting time)*

MAKES
2 dozen

The **DECIDEDLY** not-mushy messages on these **VALENTINE** sugar cookies come straight from the confectioner's mouth, but you can always slip in a few of your own original musings for a **MORE PERSONAL** touch.

INGREDIENTS

For the cookies

2½ cups flour, plus more for dusting

1 teaspoon baking powder

½ teaspoon kosher salt

1 cup sugar

¾ cup (1½ sticks) unsalted butter, softened

2 eggs, room temperature

½ teaspoon vanilla extract

For decorating

1 batch royal icing (see recipe at right)

Red gel food coloring

Blue gel food coloring

Yellow gel food coloring

Red food writer

Special equipment

Mickey Mouse cookie cutter

DIRECTIONS

1. In a small bowl, whisk together the flour, baking powder, and salt. In the bowl of a stand mixer fit with a paddle attachment and set on medium-high speed, beat the sugar and butter until light and fluffy, about 3 minutes. Add the eggs and vanilla and beat to incorporate. Reduce the mixer's speed to low and blend in the flour mixture ⅓ at a time. Do not overmix.

2. Turn the dough out onto a lightly floured surface and knead a few times. Roll it into a ball and flatten into a disk. Cover with plastic, and refrigerate 30 minutes.

3. Heat the oven to 350°F. Line two baking sheets with parchment paper. Roll out the dough to ¼-inch thickness. Use the Mickey cutter to shape the dough and arrange the cookies on the baking sheets, spacing them 2 inches apart. Gather and reroll the dough as needed.

4. Bake the cookies until set and slightly crisp, turning them once halfway through, about 12 minutes. Let the cookies cool on the pans for 5 minutes, then transfer them to a rack to cool completely.

5. Evenly divide the icing among 3 bowls. Tint each with one of the gel food colorings and place in a piping bag fit with a medium writing tip. Outline the edges of each cookie, then flood the centers to cover completely, as shown. Let the icing set.

6. Use the food writer to write the desired messages on each cookie.

ROYAL ICING

INGREDIENTS

4 cups confectioners' sugar
3 teaspoons meringue powder
2 tablespoons corn syrup

DIRECTIONS

In the bowl of a stand mixer fit with the whisk attachment, combine the sugar, meringue powder, and corn syrup with 6 tablespoons warm water. Beat on medium speed until thickened but not stiff. If the icing is too thick, add another tablespoon water; if too thin, add another tablespoon sugar.

Love Is in the Air Fairy-Tale PARFAITS

PREP
5 min

COOK
4 hr 20 min
(*includes chilling time*)

SERVES
6

From Cinderella and Prince Charming to Jack Skellington and Sally, there's no shortage of **ENCHANTED** couples in Disney narratives. This super streamlined dessert can serve as a **SWEET GESTURE** to share with someone you love on Valentine's Day or whenever the mood strikes.

INGREDIENTS

2 (3-ounce) packages blue gelatin

3 large strawberries

2 cups frozen whipped topping, thawed

DIRECTIONS

1 Prepare the gelatin according to the package directions. Trim away the top of each strawberry, then slice into hearts, as shown.

2 To assemble each parfait, adhere a few strawberry hearts to the inside of each glass, then fill the glass with uneven, alternating layers of gelatin and whipped topping. If you like, finish each parfait with a dollop of whipped topping and a strawberry heart.

CUTTING STRAWBERRIES HOW-TO

Lucky Day DOUGHNUTS

PREP
5 min

COOK
30 min

MAKES
12

Begin your **ST. PATRICK'S DAY** revelry with a breakfast made of a dozen **RAINBOWS**! In addition to golden sprinkles, each one is flanked by Mickey clouds made from **JUMBO** store-bought marshmallows. Who would **WISH** for more?

INGREDIENTS

Red food coloring

Blue food coloring

Yellow food coloring

¾ cup white frosting

12 chocolate-covered doughnuts

12 jumbo marshmallows

Gold confetti sprinkles

Special equipment

Mickey Mouse cookie cutter

DIRECTIONS

1 Use the food coloring to tint 3 tablespoons frosting in each of the following colors: red, orange, yellow, green, blue, and purple, blending colors as needed. Place each portion of frosting in a piping bag fit with a small writing tip. Pipe a rainbow onto each doughnut, as shown.

2 Halve each jumbo marshmallow crosswise, then use the Mickey cutter to shape them. Attach a pair of marshmallows to each doughnut using their sticky sides. Adhere gold confetti sprinkles as shown with the remaining frosting (a toothpick works well for this step). Keep cool until ready to serve.

CUTTING MARSHMALLOWS HOW-TO ↱

Tink's Sparkling St. Patrick's Day PETIT FOURS

PREP 5 min

COOK 30 min

MAKES 2 dozen

These two-bite cakes—sprinkled with gold stars and **PIXIE DUST** (sanding sugar)—take little more than a flick of a **WAND** to create, thanks to the help of store-bought pound cake and **FROSTING**.

INGREDIENTS

1 (16-ounce) frozen pound cake loaf

1 (16-ounce) can frosting

Green food coloring

White and gold sugar pearls

White nonpareils

Gold sanding sugar

Edible gold leaf

Gold star sprinkles

DIRECTIONS

1 Cut the pound cake into ¾-inch-thick slices, then use a mini diamond cookie cutter to shape each slice into 2 diamonds. Set a wire rack over a baking sheet.

2 Place the frosting in a microwave-safe bowl. Warm at full power for 1 minute, then stir the frosting and continue to heat in 10-second bursts until completely melted and runny. Tint with the green food coloring.

3 Working with one piece of cake at a time over the bowl of frosting, set the cake on the tines of a fork and spoon frosting over the top several times to coat it thoroughly. Transfer to a wire rack (a skewer works well for coaxing the cake off the fork). Embellish immediately with sugar pearls, nonpareils, sanding sugar, gold leaf, and gold stars. Repeat with the remaining cakes, frosting, and decorations. Let the frosting set completely. Keep cool until ready to serve.

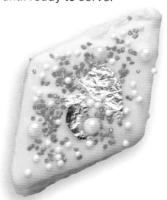

Donald's Easter CHEESE BALL

PREP
5 min

COOK
2 hr 15 min
(*includes chilling time*)

SERVES
6

Cheese and quackers anyone? Jokes aside, this **UNIQUELY** shaped hors d'oeuvre will add **PERSONALITY** to your party table.

INGREDIENTS

2¾ cups finely shredded white cheddar

12 ounces cream cheese, softened

¼ cup chopped chives

1 teaspoon Worcestershire sauce

½ teaspoon cayenne pepper sauce

Kosher salt

Black pepper

2 slices yellow cheddar

1 slice white cheddar

2 large black olives, halved

½ red bell pepper

DIRECTIONS

1 In a large bowl, combine 2 cups shredded cheddar with the cream cheese, chives, Worcestershire sauce, and cayenne pepper sauce. Season with salt and pepper. Use a sheet of plastic wrap to mold the cheese into a circle, as shown. (A small bowl works well for shaping the cheese. Just be sure it is covered with plastic so it doesn't stick.) Cover and chill until firm, about 2 hours.

2 Meanwhile, use kitchen shears to trim the yellow cheddar slices into a duck bill and the white cheddar slice into eyes, as shown. Trim the bell pepper into a bow tie.

3 Cover the cheese ball with the remaining cheddar. Transfer to a serving platter and set the eyes, bill, and bow tie in place. Set 2 olive halves in place for the pupils. Trim the other olive pieces into brows and nostrils and arrange them, as shown. Refrigerate until ready to serve with crackers.

Helpful TIP

You can make the cheese ball a day ahead: just assemble the face right before serving.

CRUDITÉ TWO WAYS

The Mickey (page 210)

The Minnie (page 211)

Whether SWEET or SAVORY, a platter full of fruits or veggies and a dunk-worthy dip is a surefire way to make any occasion merrier. Here the Mickey platter pairs a KALEIDOSCOPE of veggies with a smoky homemade hummus, while the Minnie version takes a sweeter approach with FRESH fruit and lemon mascarpone dip. Sidenote: if you can't settle on which to make, it's also okay to assemble a platter with a little bit of everything!

THE MICKEY

PREP: 15 min • COOK: 10 min • SERVES: 10

INGREDIENTS

For the smoky hummus

2 (13.5-ounce) cans chickpeas

2 cloves grated garlic

$\frac{2}{3}$ cup plus 2 tablespoons olive oil

1 teaspoon salt

6 tablespoons tahini

Juice of 1 lemon

1 tablespoon smoked paprika

For the platter

10 to 12 cups raw vegetables in various colors, whole or cut into bite-size pieces

1 small wedge or several slices your favorite cheese

$\frac{1}{2}$ baguette cut into $\frac{1}{2}$-inch-thick slices

DIRECTIONS

1 In a blender, combine all the ingredients for the hummus with $\frac{1}{4}$ cup cool water and puree until smooth. (For a creamier dip, you can add more water 1 tablespoon at a time until the desired consistency is reached.) Taste and adjust seasoning if desired. Assemble the platter as shown, using a larger bowl filled with hummus for the head and two bowls of bread for the ears, and surrounding them with the vegetables and cheese arranged in rainbow order. Keep refrigerated until ready to serve.

THE MINNIE

PREP: 15 min • COOK: 10 min • SERVES: 10

INGREDIENTS

For the lemon mascarpone dessert dip

8 ounces mascarpone

2 cups Greek yogurt

Juice of 2 lemons, plus 4 teaspoons zest

Pinch kosher salt

8 to 10 tablespoons confectioners' sugar

1 teaspoon vanilla extract

Yellow food coloring (optional)

For the platter

10 to 12 cups raw fruit in various colors, whole or cut into bite-size pieces

2 large strawberries

1 small wedge or several slices your favorite cheese

2 cups pound cake, cut into cubes

DIRECTIONS

1 In a small bowl, whisk together all the ingredients for the dessert dip. Assemble the platter as shown, using a larger bowl filled with mascarpone dip for the head and the two bowls of pound cake for the ears, and surrounding them with the fruit and cheese arranged in color blocks. Finish by cutting the strawberries into a bow shape, thread the pieces onto a toothpick, and set in place, as shown. Keep refrigerated until ready to serve.

Kitten Bow CUPCAKES

PREP
5 min

COOK
1 hr

MAKES
12

Nothing shouts **NOBILITY** more than a dessert made in your honor. With that in mind, we present a trio of cupcakes **FASHIONED** after the kittens of *The Aristocats*. The recipe includes steps for making your own cupcakes from scratch, but a mix **WOULD** work just as well.

INGREDIENTS

For the cupcakes

1½ cups flour

1 teaspoon baking powder

½ teaspoon kosher salt

½ cup unsalted butter

⅔ cup sugar

2 large eggs

2 teaspoons vanilla

¾ cup whole milk

For decorating

1 recipe candy modeling clay (see recipe at right) or 1 cup white fondant

Pink gel food coloring

Red gel food coloring

Blue gel food coloring

1 cup white frosting

Orange gel food coloring

Black gel food coloring

⅓ cup chocolate frosting

DIRECTIONS

1 Heat the oven to 350°F and line a standard muffin tin with baking cups. In a small bowl, whisk together the flour, baking powder, and salt. In the bowl of a stand mixer fit with a paddle attachment and set on medium-high speed, beat the butter and sugar until light and fluffy, about 3 minutes. Add the eggs one at a time and blend after each addition. Mix in the vanilla. Reduce the mixer's speed to low and blend in the flour mixture and milk ⅓ cup at a time, alternating between ingredients. Do not overmix.

2 Fill each baking cup ¾ full, then bake until the cupcakes are golden around the edges and a toothpick inserted in the center comes out clean, about 20 minutes. Let the cupcakes cool in the pans for 5 minutes, then transfer them to a rack to cool completely.

3 Evenly divide the candy clay into 3 portions. Knead each until softened, then tint each with a gel food coloring. Shape each portion into 4 bows, as shown. Let dry 10 minutes.

4 Meanwhile, place ½ cup white frosting in a piping bag fit with a grass tip. Put the remaining white frosting in a small bowl and tint with a few drops of orange and one drop of black food coloring. Transfer to a piping bag fit with a grass tip. Place the chocolate frosting in a piping bag fit with a small star tip.

5 Working with one frosting color at a time, cover 4 cupcakes with frosting, as shown, then top with the corresponding bow. Repeat with the remaining frosting and cupcakes. Keep cool until ready to serve.

CANDY MODELING CLAY

INGREDIENTS

1⅓ cups white candy melts

2 tablespoons plus 1 teaspoon light corn syrup

DIRECTIONS

Melt the candy according to the package directions and stir until smooth. Place the corn syrup in a heat-safe bowl. Warm in the microwave at 50 percent power for 10 seconds, then fold into the candy melts until just blended (do not overmix or it will cause the mixture to separate). Pour the mixture out onto a piece of plastic wrap. Seal and let sit at least 1 hour. Once dry, knead the candy until smooth. Keep wrapped tightly to avoid drying out the chocolate. Wrap and refrigerate if not using immediately.

July 4 Fairy Fruit PIZZA

PREP
5 min

COOK
30 min

SERVES
8

This fresh, non-savory take on pizza summons **THE MAGIC** of the fairies with its dainty appearance. Red and blue fruit work well for the Fourth, but you can also adapt the recipe by using **SEASONAL** produce for any time of year.

INGREDIENTS

For the fruit pizza

1 (16.5-ounce) roll refrigerated cookie dough

3 strawberries, thinly sliced

1 heaping cup blueberries

8 small raspberries

5 blackberries

1 small kiwifruit, peeled and sliced

For the cream cheese frosting

1 (8-ounce) package cream cheese

¼ cup (½ stick) unsalted butter

¾ teaspoon vanilla

2 cups confectioners' sugar

DIRECTIONS

1 Tear the roll of cookie dough into pieces and press into a 10-inch springform pan, as shown. To evenly flatten the surface of the dough in the pan, cover it with a sheet of parchment paper and rub until smooth. Bake according to the package directions. Let cool in the pan 5 minutes, then transfer to a rack to cool completely.

2 In a large bowl with a hand mixer set on low speed, blend together all the frosting ingredients until just combined. Increase the mixer's speed to medium and beat until light and fluffy, about 2 minutes.

3 Evenly spread the frosting over the cookie. Top with fruit arranged in flower shapes, as shown. Keep refrigerated until ready to serve.

PRESSING DOUGH HOW-TO ↷

Judy Hopps's Carrot Cake Smoothie (page 218)

HOP TO IT!

The Easter Bunny may call the shots on hiding HOLIDAY baskets, but for this collection of delights we turned to our own in-house rabbits. Pick the one that best suits the way you like to CELEBRATE the day, whether it's a spontaneous smoothie snack or a batch of make-and-share CUPCAKES.

Thumper's Mini Ice Cream Cones (page 218)

Rabbit's Carrot Patch Cupcakes (page 219)

JUDY HOPPS'S CARROT CAKE SMOOTHIE

PREP: 5 min • COOK: 5 min • SERVES: 2

INGREDIENTS

1 frozen banana

3 to 4 pitted dates

1 cup shredded carrots (about 2 medium)

1 cup full-fat coconut milk

¼ teaspoon ground cinnamon

2 pinches nutmeg

Whipped cream, for garnishing

½ graham cracker

3 tablespoons toasted coconut

DIRECTIONS

1 In a blender, combine the banana, dates, carrot, coconut milk, cinnamon, and nutmeg with 1 cup ice, and process until smooth. Evenly divide the drink between two glasses. Top each with whipped cream and half the cracker and coconut. Serve immediately.

THUMPER'S MINI ICE CREAM CONES

PREP: 5 min • COOK: 30 min • SERVES: 6

INGREDIENTS

2 tablespoons black candy melts

⅓ cup white candy melts

⅓ cup pink candy melts

1½ cups vanilla ice cream

6 mini cones

1 tablespoon gray or silver sprinkles

12 mini chocolate chips

6 pink jelly beans

1 tablespoon chocolate sprinkles

DIRECTIONS

1 Line a baking sheet with parchment paper. Combine the black and white candy melts in a heat-safe bowl and melt according to the package directions. Stir to blend evenly, then transfer to a piping bag fit with a large writing tip. Repeat with the pink candy melts.

2 Use the gray candy to pipe a 2-inch ear onto the prepared baking sheet. Repeat to make 11 more ears. Pipe a pink center onto each ear and let the candy set.

3 To serve, scoop vanilla ice cream into a cone and cover the top lightly with gray sprinkles. Top with two candy ears, a pair of chocolate chip eyes, a jelly bean nose, and chocolate sprinkle whiskers, as shown. Repeat with the remaining ice cream, cones, and decorative ingredients. Serve immediately.

RABBIT'S CARROT PATCH CUPCAKES

PREP: 5 min • COOK: 25 min • MAKES: 2 dozen

INGREDIENTS

24 orange fruit chew candies

2 green licorice twists

24 unfrosted mini chocolate cupcakes

1 cup chocolate frosting

6 chocolate sandwich cookies, crushed

DIRECTIONS

1 Mold each fruit chew candy into a carrot shape. (If the candy is too hard to shape, it can be placed in the microwave for 5 seconds.) Snip the licorice into 1-inch lengths. Halve each lengthwise, then fray the end, as shown. Use a toothpick to bore a hole in the top of each candy carrot and insert a licorice piece.

2 Working with one cupcake at a time, cover the top with frosting, then sprinkle with cookie crumbs. Repeat with the remaining cupcakes. Insert a candy carrot into the top of each cupcake. Keep cool until ready to serve.

CANDY CARROT HOW-TO

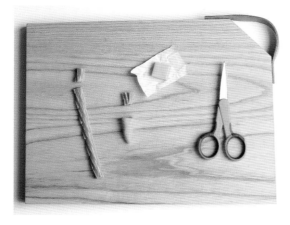

Sugar Skull COOKIES

PREP
5 min

COOK
1 hr 30 min
(includes
setting time)

MAKES
18

Chocolate-cinnamon cutout cookies are the base for this **COLORFULLY** decorated **DESSERT** inspired by the movie *Coco*. For the best results, let them cool **COMPLETELY** before decorating so the icing stays in place and sets.

INGREDIENTS

For the Mexican chocolate cutout cookies

2 cups flour, plus more for dusting

$2/3$ cup dark cocoa powder

½ teaspoon ground cinnamon

½ teaspoon kosher salt

¾ cup (1½ sticks) butter, softened

1 cup sugar

1 egg, room temperature

½ teaspoon vanilla

For decorating

1 batch royal icing (see recipe page 199)

Black gel food coloring

Orange gel food coloring

Pink gel food coloring

Blue gel food coloring

Special equipment

Skull cookie cutter

DIRECTIONS

1 In a small bowl, whisk together the flour, cocoa powder, cinnamon, and salt. In the bowl of a stand mixer fit with a paddle attachment and set on medium-high speed, beat the butter and sugar until light and fluffy, about 3 minutes. Add the egg and vanilla and beat to incorporate. Reduce the mixer's speed to low and blend in the flour mixture ⅓ at a time. Do not overmix.

2 Turn the dough out onto a lightly floured surface and knead. Roll into a ball and flatten into a disk. Cover with plastic and refrigerate 30 minutes.

3 Heat the oven to 350°F. Line two baking sheets with parchment paper. Roll out the dough to ¼-inch thickness. Shape the dough with a skull cookie cutter, and arrange 2 inches apart on the baking sheets. Gather and reroll the dough as needed.

4 Bake the cookies until set and slightly crisp, turning them halfway through, about 12 minutes. Let cool on the baking sheets 5 minutes, then transfer to a rack to cool completely.

5 Place 1 cup of the icing in a piping bag fit with a medium writing tip. Outline the edges of each cookie, then flood the centers to cover completely. Let the icing set.

6 Evenly divide the remaining frosting among 4 cups. Tint each with a gel food coloring and place in a piping bag fit with a very small writing tip. Use each color to decorate the cookies, as shown, allowing the layered areas to set before adding another color. Let the icing dry completely before serving.

Jack's Chocolate-Topped RICE CAKES

PREP
5 min

COOK
30 min
(includes setting time)

SERVES
6

As the name suggests, these **SWEET** and salty cakes are made with just a few **SIMPLE** ingredients. The recipe easily doubles—or even triples—if your planning on **SHARING** with a large group.

INGREDIENTS

1½ cups white candy melts

2 teaspoons vegetable oil

6 plain rice cakes

⅓ cup chocolate chips

DIRECTIONS

1 Combine the candy melts and vegetable oil in a microwave-safe bowl and melt according to the package directions. Stir until smooth, then transfer to a piping bag fit with a large writing tip. Pipe a layer of candy onto each rice cake and smooth out with a spoon or offset spatula. Let the candy set.

2 Place the chocolate chips in a microwave-safe bowl and melt according to the package directions. Transfer to a piping bag fit with a small writing tip and pipe eyes and a mouth onto each rice cake, as shown. Let the chocolate set. Keep cool until ready to serve.

Ingredient SWAP

We chose white candy melts for this recipe due to their bright color, but they can be replaced with white chocolate if you prefer.

Nutcracker Cookies (page 226)

Frozen Snowflakes (page 227)

GINGERBREAD FIVE WAYS

Be the **STAR** of your holiday baking swap by replacing traditional Mr. and Ms. cookies with a Disney-fied design. Aside from their **UNEXPECTED** shapes, these cookies earn extra points for their crisp-tender texture and balanced flavor. For each, follow our main recipe for making a batch of dough, then jump to your **FAVORITE** design and follow the instructions.

Baymax Cookies
(page 227)

Minnie Cookies
(page 227)

Mickey Cookies
(page 227)

BASIC GINGERBREAD DOUGH

PREP: 5 min • COOK: 1 hr 45 min (includes chilling time)
MAKES: 3 to 4 dozen

INGREDIENTS

4 cups flour, plus more for dusting

2 teaspoons ground ginger

1 teaspoon ground cinnamon

½ teaspoon ground cloves

1 teaspoon baking soda

½ teaspoon kosher salt

1 cup (2 sticks) unsalted butter, room temperature

1 cup dark brown sugar, packed

1 egg, room temperature

½ cup molasses

DIRECTIONS

1 Heat the oven to 375°F and line two baking sheets with parchment paper. In a medium bowl, whisk together the flour, ginger, cinnamon, cloves, baking soda, and salt.

2 In the bowl of a stand mixer fit with a paddle attachment and set on medium-high speed, cream the butter and sugar until light and fluffy, about 3 minutes. Add the egg and blend to incorporate. Add the molasses and blend once more. Reduce the mixer's speed to low and blend in the flour mixture, ⅓ at a time.

3 On a lightly floured surface, knead the dough a few times, then halve it. Roll each portion into a ball, flatten it into a disk, wrap in plastic, and refrigerate 1 hour.

4 On a lightly floured surface, roll one portion of the dough out to ¼-inch thickness. Use the cookie cutter listed in your chosen design to shape the dough. Arrange them on the baking sheets, spacing them 2 inches apart. Gather and reroll the dough as needed.

5 Bake the cookies until slightly crisp around the edges and fully set, turning them halfway through, about 10 minutes. Let them cool on the baking sheets 5 minutes, then transfer to a rack to cool completely. Repeat cutting and baking steps for the second portion of dough, then proceed to your chosen design and follow the instructions for decorating.

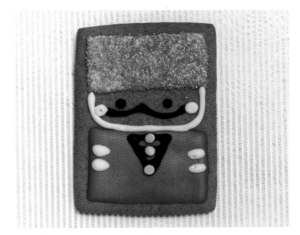

NUTCRACKER COOKIES

PREP: 5 min • COOK: 1 hr • MAKES: About 3 dozen

INGREDIENTS

1 batch royal icing (see recipe page 199)

Red gel food coloring

Black gel food coloring

Yellow gel food coloring

Pink gel food coloring

¼ cup gold sanding sugar

2 tablespoons gold confetti sprinkles

For shaping: **3½-inch rectangular cookie cutter**

DIRECTIONS

1 Evenly divide the icing among five small bowls. Tint four of the bowls with one of the gel food colors each. Transfer each portion of icing, along with the remaining white icing to a piping bag fit with a small writing tip.

2 Working with one cookie at a time, use the white icing to outline the hat at the top of the cookie, as shown, then flood the center with more icing and cover with gold sanding sugar. Repeat with the remaining cookies.

3 Outline and flood the bottom of each cookie with the red icing to add a suit, as shown. Let the icing set for 15 minutes, then pipe on the remaining details with the black, yellow, and pink icing. Finish by adding gold confetti sprinkle buttons to each cookie.

FROZEN SNOWFLAKES

PREP: 5 min • COOK: 45 min • MAKES: About 4 dozen

INGREDIENTS

1 batch royal icing (see recipe page 199)

Blue gel food coloring

2 tablespoons sparkling sugar

1 tablespoon blue sugar pearls

1 tablespoon white sugar pearls

For shaping: 2- to 3-inch round cookie cutter

DIRECTIONS

1 Place half the icing in a small bowl. Tint with blue food coloring. Place each portion of icing in a piping bag fit with a small writing tip.

2 Use the white icing to draw a snowflake on a cookie, as shown. Embellish with sparkling sugar or blue sugar pearls. Repeat with half the cookies. Decorate the remaining cookies with the blue icing, leftover sparkling sugar, and white sugar pearls. Let the icing set before serving.

BAYMAX COOKIES

PREP: 5 min • COOK: 1 hr (includes setting time)
MAKES: About 4 dozen

INGREDIENTS

1 batch royal icing (see recipe page 199)

Black gel food coloring

For shaping: Oval cookie cutter

DIRECTIONS

1 Place ¼ cup icing in a small bowl. Tint with the black food coloring. Transfer each portion of icing to a piping bag fit with a small writing tip.

2 Use the white icing to outline and flood each cookie. Let the icing set 20 minutes, then use the black icing to draw eyes on each cookie. Let the icing fully set before serving.

MICKEY and MINNIE COOKIES

PREP: 5 min • COOK: 45 min • MAKES: About 4 dozen

INGREDIENTS

1 batch royal icing (see recipe page 199)

Pink gel food coloring

Red gel food coloring

¼ cup pink fondant

1 tablespoon white sugar pearls

1 cup yellow chocolate gem candies

For shaping: Mickey Mouse cookie cutter

DIRECTIONS

1 Evenly divide the icing into three portions and place each in a small bowl. Use the food coloring to tint one bowl pink and another red. Transfer each portion to a piping bag fit with a small writing tip.

2 Use the white icing to outline the strip of fur at the center of each cookie, as shown, then flood the center with more icing.

3 To decorate the Minnie cookies, shape the fondant into bows for half the cookies, as shown, then use the white icing to attach them. Outline and flood the bottom of each cookie with pink icing, then dot with white sugar pearls.

4 For the Mickey cookies, outline and flood the bottom with red icing, then attach two yellow chocolate gems. Let the icing set on all the cookies before serving.

EVERYTHING for the HOLIDAYS : 227

Dumbo's Big Top Candy Cane CUPCAKES

PREP
5 min

COOK
35 min

MAKES
12

The secret to making these holiday treats a main **ATTRACTION** is their lofty tops. To achieve this, start by baking your cupcakes at 400°F until the tops have risen to the **DESIRED** height, then reduce the oven temperature to finish baking.

INGREDIENTS

12 sour red fruit strips

12 green gumdrops

12 unfrosted vanilla cupcakes

1 cup white frosting

Special equipment

Washi tape

12 toothpicks

DIRECTIONS

1 Cut a 3-inch length of washi tape. Center and fold the tape over the top of a toothpick, as shown. Trim the end of the tape into a flag and break off 1 inch of the toothpick. Repeat with the remaining toothpicks and tape.

2 Cut each fruit strip into 5 triangles, as shown, then set aside. Insert a flag into the top of each gumdrop.

3 Working with one cupcake at a time, cover it with frosting, then arrange 5 candy wedges around the top, as shown. Top with a gumdrop flag in the center (use more frosting to adhere it if needed). Repeat with the remaining cupcakes and ingredients.

FLAG HOW-TO ↪

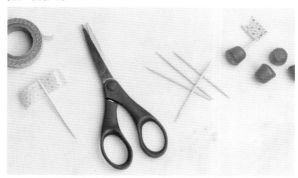

Candle CAKES

PREP
5 min

COOK
2 hr 10 min
(*includes chilling time*)

SERVES
8 to 10

These **TOWERS** may look like real candles, but there's nothing here other than vanilla **FROSTING** and sponge cake. Light them up at the end of a winter **HOLIDAY** meal for a dramatic finish.

INGREDIENTS

1 (15-ounce) box your favorite cake mix

3 (16-ounce) cans white frosting

3 birthday candles

Fresh rosemary sprigs, for garnish (optional)

Fresh cranberries, for garnish (optional)

Special equipment

Cookie cutter

DIRECTIONS

1 Bake the cake mix in two 9-inch cake pans according to the package directions. Remove from the pans and let cool completely on a rack.

2 Use a 3- to 4-inch cookie cutter to shape each cake into 4 circles. You will need a total of 3 equal-sized cakes for each larger candle, and 2 equal-sized cakes for the smallest candle. Trim a small square of parchment paper to fit underneath each cake. To assemble each pillar, stack identical layers of cake on a sheet of parchment, as noted, adding frosting in between. Use the remaining frosting from the first can to cover each cake with a thin layer and refrigerate until set, about 1 hour.

3 Use another can of frosting to generously cover each pillar. Transfer the cakes to your serving platter, remove the parchment, and arrange as desired.

4 Place 1 cup of frosting from the remaining can in a microwave-safe bowl and warm at full power for 1 minute. Stir and continue to heat in 10-second bursts until completely melted and runny. Let cool slightly, then drizzle around the top of each cake to create a drippy appearance. Let the frosting set. If desired, garnish your serving platter with rosemary and fresh cranberries. Just before serving, insert a candle into the top of each cake, as shown, and light.

Chapter

1

EASY TREATS

SOMETIMES IT'S BEST TO JUST KEEP THINGS SIMPLE, AS IN THREE STEPS OR LESS.

While the whole book is filled with easy ideas, the ones here are some of the most uncomplicated of them all. If you're planning for a party, you can make things even more streamlined by opting for a treat you can do ahead (see Under the Sea Lollipops, page 255). Or skip the prep, set up a station, and let your guests get in on the fun by making their own (see Mickey Split, page 251).

Captain Hook BROWNIE BITES

PREP
5 min

COOK
25 min

MAKES
12

Reel in the gang with a **CHOCOLATY DELIGHT** that recalls the most villainous character in Never Land.

INGREDIENTS

⅓ cup white candy melts

6 black candy melts

1½ cups white frosting

Red gel food coloring

12 store-bought brownie bites

DIRECTIONS

1 Line a baking sheet with parchment paper. Combine the candy melts in a small microwave-safe bowl, and melt according to the package directions. Transfer the candy to a piping bag fit with a small writing tip, then pipe 12 hook shapes onto the prepared pan. Let the candy set.

2 Meanwhile, place ½ cup frosting in a small bowl and tint with red food coloring. Transfer it to a piping bag fit with a large round tip. Place the remaining frosting in a piping bag fit with a large star tip.

3 Pipe a large dollop of red frosting onto the top of each brownie bite by centering the piping tip atop the brownie, holding it ¼ inch from the surface, and pushing the frosting out so that it spreads to form a circle, as shown. Repeat the technique to add a dollop of white frosting to each brownie. Finish by adding a candy hook to each. Keep cool until ready to serve.

Frozen POPS

PREP
5 min

COOK
9 hr
(includes freezing time)

MAKES
10

These **REFRESHING POPS** get their ombré look from a **NO-SWEAT** layering technique. It requires an extra freezing step, but the effort involved is mostly in waiting until **THEY'RE READY TO EAT**!

INGREDIENTS

1¼ cups blue sports drink

1¼ cups purple sports drink

Special equipment

Wooden treat sticks

DIRECTIONS

1 Pour the blue sports drink into a small, freezer-safe baking dish. Pour the purple sports drink into another dish and freeze both until solid, about 3 hours.

2 Use the end of a butter knife to break each frozen drink into small pieces. Evenly divide the blue pieces among 10 ice-pop molds, followed by the purple pieces. Top off each mold with water, add a wooden treat stick, and freeze until solid, about 6 hours.

M and M MILK TOPPERS

PREP
5 min

COOK
25 min

MAKES
8

It's **TEMPTING** to cut the holes in the center of the cookies before they bake, but don't—they'll likely **SHRINK** or close altogether in the process (trust us, we've tried). If you don't own a set of **MILK BOTTLES**, you can easily find them online or at a craft store for $1 or $2 each.

INGREDIENTS

Flour, for dusting

½ (16-ounce) roll store-bought chocolate chip cookie dough

¼ cup white frosting

8 large red heart sprinkles

4 large red square or confetti sprinkles

Milk for serving

Special equipment

2- to 3-inch Mickey Mouse cookie cutter

Drinking straws

Milk bottles (optional)

DIRECTIONS

1 Heat the oven to 350°F. Line a baking sheet with parchment paper. On a lightly floured surface, roll out the dough. Use the Mickey Mouse cookie cutter to cut 8 shapes from the dough. Transfer to the baking sheet and bake according to the package directions.

2 Let the cookies cool 2 minutes, then use a drinking straw to cut a hole in the center of each one. Let cool completely.

3 Use a toothpick and frosting to attach a red sprinkle bow to four of the cookies, as shown. To serve, fill a milk bottle or small-mouth glass with milk. Set the cookie on top and thread a straw through the center opening.

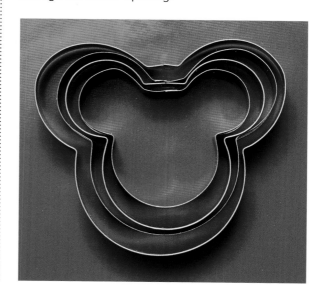

Sleeping Beauty S'MORES

PREP
5 min

COOK
35 min

MAKES
12

The **DREAMIEST** part of these marshmallow sweets is that they don't require a flame. Instead, the graham cracker base is topped with marshmallow, then **GENEROUSLY COATED** with a blanket of melted chocolate.

INGREDIENTS

6 graham crackers, halved

12 large marshmallows, halved lengthwise

12 mini vanilla wafer cookies

Black food writer

Pink food writer

1½ cups purple candy melts

3 teaspoons vegetable oil

Purple nonpareils

½ cup yellow candy melts

12 crown sprinkles

MARSHMALLOW AND
VANILLA WAFER HOW-TO ⤵

DIRECTIONS

1 Arrange two marshmallow halves sticky-side-down on each graham cracker, as shown. Use the food writers to draw a pair of black eyes and pink cheeks on each vanilla wafer.

2 In a small, microwave-safe bowl, combine the purple candy melts with 2 teaspoons vegetable oil. Melt according to the package directions. Use a toothpick and a bit of the melted candy to attach the marshmallow pillow and cookie face to each graham cracker, as shown. Working with one s'more at a time, drizzle 2 tablespoons of the melted candy over the bottom marshmallow, then scatter immediately with nonpareils. Repeat with the remaining candy.

3 In a small, microwave-safe bowl, combine the yellow candy melts with the remaining teaspoon of vegetable oil. Melt according to the package directions. Transfer to a piping bag fit with a small writing tip. Working with one treat at a time, pipe hair onto the head, as shown, then attach a sprinkle crown. Let the candy set before serving.

Baklava BITES

PREP
5 min

COOK
30 min

MAKES
15

Baking with **WHOLE** phyllo sheets can be a bit fussy, so we've **SWAPPED** them in this recipe with easier-to-work-with phyllo cups. You can find them in the **FROZEN** section of most grocery stores.

INGREDIENTS

1 (2-ounce) package phyllo cups

½ cup roasted walnuts

½ cup roasted pistachios

Heaping ½ teaspoon orange zest

3 tablespoons sugar

½ teaspoon ground cinnamon

¼ teaspoon kosher salt

2 tablespoons unsalted butter, melted

2 tablespoons honey

DIRECTIONS

1 Heat the oven to 350°F. Arrange the phyllo cups on a baking sheet. In a food processor, combine the nuts, orange zest, 2 tablespoons sugar, and the cinnamon, salt, and butter. Pulse until the nuts are coarsely chopped.

2 Fill each phyllo cup with the nut mixture. Bake until the cups are golden brown, about 20 minutes.

3 While the baklava cooks, combine the remaining tablespoon sugar, the honey, and ⅓ cup water in a saucepan over medium-high heat. Bring to a boil, then lower the heat and let simmer until reduced by half. As soon as the sweets are removed from the oven, spoon 1 teaspoon of the syrup into each cup. Let cool before serving.

Sand Dollar COOKIES

PREP
5 min

COOK
45 min

MAKES
2 dozen

Amidst all the **TREASURES** found in Ariel's **SECRET** grotto, you'd likely find at least a few aquatic creatures, including ones that resemble these **FROSTED** cookies. Enjoy them on your own **OCEANSIDE** excursion or your next pool party.

INGREDIENTS

1 (16-ounce) package sugar cookie dough

1 batch royal icing (see recipe page 199)

⅓ cup toasted almond slices

DIRECTIONS

1 Heat the oven to 350°F and line two baking sheets with parchment paper. Roll the dough out to ¼-inch thickness and use a 3-inch round cutter to shape the dough into circles. Arrange the rounds on a cookie sheet, spacing them 2 inches apart. Place in the freezer for 10 minutes.

2 Bake the cookies according to the package directions, then let cool completely. Working with one cookie at a time, cover the top with royal icing, leaving a small border. Arrange 5 almond slices on top as shown. Repeat with the remaining cookies and icing. Let the icing set completely before serving.

Bare Necessities CHOCOLATE COINS

PREP
5 min

COOK
30 min

MAKES
About
3 dozen

DOTTED with tropical fruit and nuts, these CONFECTIONS have all the ingredients a bear like Baloo would want to SNACK on, except for the insects! We're partial to DARK CHOCOLATE, but you can also make the coins with white or milk chocolate if you prefer.

INGREDIENTS

1 (11-ounce) bag high-quality dark chocolate chips

1½ cups chopped toppings such as toasted coconut, dried pineapple, toasted cashews, roasted pistachios, crystallized ginger, dried banana, and freeze-dried strawberries

DIRECTIONS

1 Line a baking sheet with parchment paper and place your chosen toppings in bowls.

2 Place the chocolate in a microwave-safe bowl and melt according to the package directions. Transfer it to a piping bag fit with a medium writing tip or to a freezer-weight zip-top bag and snip the corner. Pipe a few 2-inch buttons onto the parchment and decorate immediately with toppings. Repeat with the remaining chocolate and toppings, piping and decorating just a few at a time so the candy doesn't harden before embellishments are added. Let the chocolate harden before serving.

Mickey Split (page 251)

JUST ADD EARS

Aside from Sleeping Beauty Castle, there are few things more ICONIC than the mouse's OVERSIZED ears. You can find them on a hat or a headband at any Disney gift shop, or tucked away in UNEXPECTED places throughout the theme parks on Hidden Mickeys. Here they appear on three no-cook desserts you can WHIP UP in minutes.

Chocolate-Dipped Strawberries (page 250)

Mickey Cookie Pretzel Bark (page 250)

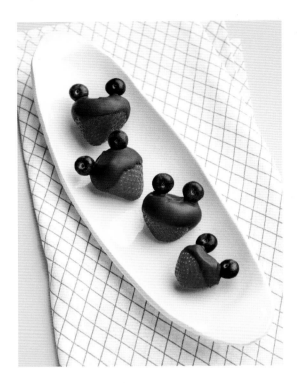

CHOCOLATE-DIPPED STRAWBERRIES

PREP: 5 min • COOK: 15 min • MAKES: 12

INGREDIENTS

⅔ cup high-quality dark chocolate chips

1 teaspoon vegetable oil

12 strawberries, leaves removed

24 blueberries

DIRECTIONS

1 Line a baking sheet with parchment paper. Combine the chocolate and vegetable oil in a microwave-safe bowl and melt according to the package directions. Dip the top of a strawberry into the chocolate, then top with two blueberry ears, as shown. Place on the baking sheet. Repeat with the remaining berries and chocolate. Let the chocolate set before serving.

MICKEY COOKIE PRETZEL BARK

PREP: 5 min • COOK: 15 min • MAKES: 1 large batch

INGREDIENTS

12 ounces white candy melts

2 teaspoons vegetable oil

8 mini chocolate sandwich cookies, pulled apart and with the filling removed

32 brown chocolate gem candies

Small handful mini pretzels

4 teaspoons red, black, yellow, and/or star sprinkles

DIRECTIONS

1 Line a baking sheet with parchment paper. Combine the candy melts and vegetable oil in a microwave-safe bowl and melt according to the package directions. Pour it out onto the prepared pan. Use a small offset spatula to spread it into a ¼-inch-thick rectangle.

2 Press the cookies into the candy and add a pair of chocolate gem ears to each, as shown. Next, add the pretzels and press them in place. Finish by scattering on the sprinkles. Let the candy set before serving.

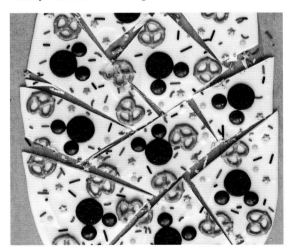

MICKEY SPLIT

PREP: 5 min • COOK: 10 min • SERVES: 2

INGREDIENTS

¾ cup raspberries

1 banana, halved crosswise

Chocolate ice cream

Chocolate syrup

4 of your favorite chocolate cookies

Whipped cream

1 tablespoon sprinkle mix (we used red, black, and yellow)

2 maraschino cherries with stems

DIRECTIONS

1 Evenly divide the raspberries between 2 parfait glasses. Halve each banana portion and add it to the glass, as shown. Place a large scoop of ice cream in each glass. Drizzle with chocolate syrup. Insert a pair of cookie ears into the scoop of ice cream, then top with whipped cream. Finish by scattering half the sprinkles onto each sundae and adding a cherry on top. Serve immediately.

Olaf SUNDAE

PREP
5 min

COOK
30 min
(includes setting time for candy)

SERVES
1

Take a **SUNDAE BAR** to the next level by setting up a **STATION** for everyone to make their own Olaf. To keep things **STREAMLINED**, we recommend assembling the faces ahead of time, then setting them out with the other ingredients. This recipe makes one sundae.

INGREDIENTS

1 orange fruit chew candy

⅓ cup white candy melts

2 candy eyes

2 scoops vanilla ice cream

Edible black marker

2 pretzel sticks

Blue sprinkles

DIRECTIONS

1 Line a small plate with parchment paper. Mold the orange fruit chew candy into the shape of Olaf's nose. Melt the candy melts according to the package directions. Spoon a bit onto the parchment paper, then use the back of the spoon to spread into the shape of Olaf's head. Attach the candy eyes and fruit chew nose, as shown, then let the candy set.

2 Use the edible marker to draw Olaf's mouth. Stack the ice cream scoops in an ice cream dish. Add pretzel stick arms and Olaf's head, as shown. Garnish with blue sprinkles. Serve immediately.

Under the Sea LOLLIPOPS

PREP
5 min

COOK
20 min
(includes
cooling time)

MAKES
6

Making these **POPS** doesn't require much effort, but you should make sure **EVERYTHING** is ready to go when the candy comes out of the oven. You'll need to work fast to **DECORATE** them before the candy cools.

INGREDIENTS

12 blue hard candies

6 green hard candies

Fish-shaped and star-shaped sprinkles

1 teaspoon white nonpareils

Special equipment

6 (4-inch) lollipop sticks

DIRECTIONS

1 Line a baking sheet with parchment paper and heat the oven to 275°F. Arrange the candies on the pan in groups of three, with two blue and one green hard candy in each set, as shown (the pieces should be touching one another).

2 Ready the lollipop sticks. Place the candies in the oven until fully melted, about 10 minutes. Working quickly (and with caution, since the candy will be very hot), press a lollipop stick into each pool of melted candy and twist gently to cover the stick. Sprinkle each pop with nonpareils, as shown. Finish by pressing a few fish-shaped and star-shaped sprinkles into each. If the candy hardens as you're working, it can be returned to the oven for 1 minute. Let the candy cool completely before wrapping or serving.

CANDY ARRANGEMENT HOW-TO

Minnie's Roasted STRAWBERRY PARFAITS

PREP
5 min

COOK
35 min
(includes cooling time)

MAKES
4

Placing **BERRIES** in the oven adds depth of flavor and creates a **JUICY** syrup that's perfect for topping all sorts of **INDULGENCES**. Pairing them with plain Greek yogurt and granola gives this parfait a wholesome **TWIST**.

INGREDIENTS

4 cups strawberries (about 1 pound), halved

2 tablespoons brown sugar

¼ teaspoon vanilla extract

Generous pinch kosher salt

2 cups plain Greek yogurt

1⅓ cups plain granola

DIRECTIONS

1 Heat the oven to 375°F. In an 8-inch baking dish, stir together the strawberries, sugar, vanilla, and salt until the fruit is evenly coated. Roast the strawberries until they've softened and released their juices, about 20 minutes. Let cool 10 minutes.

2 To assemble each parfait, spoon ¼ cup yogurt into the bottom of a glass. Add a layer of strawberries, with their juices, and top with a few tablespoons granola. Repeat the layers, then assemble 3 more parfaits using the remaining ingredients. Eat immediately.

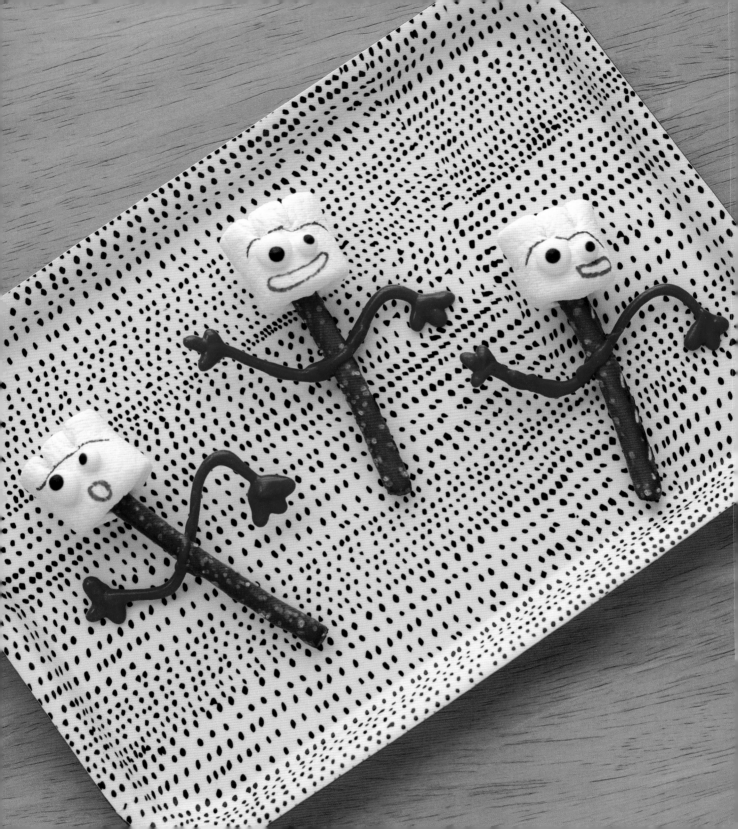

Forky PRETZELS

PREP
5 min

COOK
20 min

MAKES
12

These easy-to-assemble **SNACKS** are a little **SWEET**, a little salty, and just as quirky as the companion Bonnie **CREATED** on her first day of kindergarten.

INGREDIENTS

⅔ cup red candy melts

1 teaspoon vegetable oil

12 small pretzel rods

12 large marshmallows

12 medium candy eyes

12 small candy eyes

1 tablespoon white frosting

Red food writer

Blue food writer

DIRECTIONS

1 Line two baking sheets with parchment paper. Combine the candy melts and vegetable oil in a microwave-safe bowl and melt according to the package directions. Transfer the candy to a piping bag fit with a large writing tip.

2 Pipe a pair of arms by making one continuous line, as shown. Center a pretzel stick and press it in place on top. Add a line of candy on top of the pretzel to secure it in place. Repeat with the remaining candy and pretzels. Let the candy set.

3 Meanwhile, use kitchen shears to make 3 small snips in the top of each marshmallow. Use the frosting and a toothpick to attach one large and one small candy eye to each marshmallow, as shown. Add a red brow and blue mouth with the food writers. Slide a head onto each pretzel body. Keep cool until ready to serve.

ARMS HOW-TO ↝

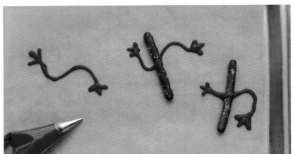

Chapter

8

BIRTHDAYS
and SWEET OCCASIONS

IT'S TIME TO PARTY, and YOU NEED SOMETHING SPECIAL THAT WILL WOW but not OVERWHELM as you put it all together. While the recipes here range from easy assembly (see *Up*-Cakes, page 281) to more elaborate projects (see *Sleeping Beauty* Doughnut Cake, page 266), none is very complicated. For longer recipes, consider recruiting an extra set of hands to help so you can speed ahead to the important part—celebrating.

Maleficent Triple Chocolate SANDWICH COOKIES

PREP
5 min

COOK
45 min

MAKES
12 cookies

MESMERIZE chocolate lovers with a spellbinding SWEET! These cookies come together like magic with the help of mostly store-bought ingredients and feature CHOCOLATE both inside and out.

INGREDIENTS

- ⅓ cup high-quality dark chocolate chips
- ⅓ cup green candy melts
- 24 plain chocolate wafer cookies
- ½ cup your favorite chocolate frosting
- 12 jumbo heart sprinkles

DIRECTIONS

1 Line a baking sheet with parchment paper. Melt the chocolate chips according to the package directions and transfer to a piping bag fit with a small writing tip. Pipe 12 sets of horns, as shown, onto the parchment. Let the chocolate set.

2 Meanwhile, in a small, heat-safe bowl, melt the candy melts according to the package directions. Place in a piping bag fit with a small writing tip and pipe the outline of Maleficent's face onto 12 of the cookies. Let set 3 minutes. Working with one cookie at a time, flood the center of the face with more candy and quickly place a heart sprinkle along the bottom, as shown. Repeat with the remaining candy and sprinkles. Let set completely.

3 Spread 2 teaspoons frosting onto each of the remaining cookies. Press a set of chocolate horns into the frosting along top edge of the cookie, then sandwich with a cookie face.

Lightning McQueen CAKE

PREP
5 min

COOK
2 hr 15 min
(*includes chilling time*)

SERVES
About 10

This **SHOWROOM-WORTHY** layer cake is the perfect centerpiece for a *Cars*-themed **BIRTHDAY**, with the added bonus of a more fast-paced assembly than its appearance might **SUGGEST**. If you can't find chocolate-covered snack cakes for the wheels, chocolate doughnuts are a **YUMMY** substitute.

INGREDIENTS

Cooking spray

1 (15-ounce) vanilla cake mix

3 cups white frosting

Red food coloring

Yellow food coloring

4 round chocolate-covered snack cakes

White chocolate bar

2 black candy melts

3 pretzel dipping sticks

2 vanilla wafer cookies

DIRECTIONS

1 Coat two 8- or 9-inch round cake pans with cooking spray. Prepare the cake mix according to the package directions and evenly divide the batter between the two pans. Bake as directed. Let cool in the pan 10 minutes, then turn out onto a rack to cool completely.

2 Tint $2\frac{1}{2}$ cups of the frosting with the red food coloring and place it in a piping bag fit with a large writing tip. (If you're not able to fit all the frosting in the bag, keep the extra covered with plastic.) Tint half the remaining frosting with the yellow food coloring. Cover it, along with the remaining white frosting, and set aside.

3 Set one cake on a baking sheet and pipe a layer of red frosting on the top. Spread evenly, then top with the remaining cake. Pipe and spread a thin layer of red frosting all over the cake and refrigerate 30 minutes.

4 Transfer the cake to a serving platter. Cover evenly with the remaining red frosting. Press on the chocolate snack cake wheels, as shown. Trim the white chocolate bar into a small rectangle for the windshield. Use the white frosting to attach two black candy melt eyes. Slide the pretzel rods at an angle into the center of the cake, as shown, then prop up the chocolate windshield in front. Pipe a line of red frosting around the edge of the windshield. Trim a piece of the remaining white chocolate into a mouth and press in place. To finish, cover each vanilla wafer with yellow frosting and attach.

Sleeping Beauty
DOUGHNUT CAKE

PREP
5 min

COOK
1 hr 10 min

SERVES
7

The **TOPSY-TURVY** layers of this lofty cake are impressive, but even the good fairy Fauna could pull it off. Making it is all about the **ASSEMBLY**—no baking required!—and some artful, but easy dipping and **FROSTING** action.

INGREDIENTS

2 (16-ounce) cans vanilla frosting

7 plain cake doughnuts

Blue food coloring

Yellow food coloring

$\frac{1}{3}$ cup chocolate chips

1 pretzel rod

2 large marshmallows

Pink candles

DIRECTIONS

1 Set a wire rack over a baking sheet. Place the frosting from 1 can in a microwave-safe bowl. Warm at full power for 1 minute. Stir the frosting and continue to heat in 10-second bursts until completely melted and runny. Double-dip the doughnuts in the frosting and place on the rack to let the frosting set.

2 Combine 1 cup of frosting from the second can with any remaining frosting in the bowl. Heat once more as described in Step 1. Blend in several drops of blue food coloring, then transfer to a piping bag fit with a small round tip. Pipe drips onto the doughnuts, as shown. Use a toothpick to smooth any clumps of frosting as needed. Let set.

3 Meanwhile, melt the chocolate chips according to the package directions. Use a pastry brush or mini spatula to coat the pretzel rod with chocolate, then place on a sheet of parchment paper to let the chocolate set.

4 Use frosting to secure a doughnut to your serving platter. Stack the doughnuts slightly askew, as shown. If needed, use bamboo skewers to secure the doughnuts as they are stacked. Simply poke a skewer through several doughnuts to hold them in place and trim the end to conceal.

5 Blend the remaining white frosting with several drops of yellow food coloring. Transfer half the frosting to a piping bag fit with a small star tip. Pipe bunting around the top doughnut and dots of frosting where the candles will be placed.

6 To construct the broomstick, make a slit in the top of one of the marshmallows. Use frosting to attach the uncut end to the other marshmallow. Fit the tip of the pretzel rod inside the slit marshmallow, then position the other end of the pretzel between the top two doughnuts, as shown. Attach the base of the marshmallow stack to the serving platter, then use a grass piping tip and the remaining yellow frosting to pipe lines over the marshmallows for the straw of the broom.

Inside Out CAKE BITES

PREP
5 min

COOK
1 hr

MAKES
25 cake bites

Just like the **MOVIE**, each color in these little cakes represents a different **EMOTION**. We hereby give you permission to share and eat your **FEELINGS**.

INGREDIENTS

1 cup flour

¾ cup sugar

2 teaspoons baking powder

1 large egg

½ cup buttermilk

⅓ cup sour cream

¼ cup canola or vegetable oil

2 teaspoons vanilla extract

½ cup rainbow sprinkles

Red, yellow, green, blue, and purple sugar pearls, sprinkles, or candies

2 cups vanilla frosting

DIRECTIONS

1 Heat the oven to 350°F. Line an 8-inch square baking pan with parchment paper, letting it hang over the edges slightly.

2 In a large bowl, whisk together the flour, sugar, and baking powder. In a small bowl, whisk together the egg, buttermilk, sour cream, oil, and vanilla. Combine the wet and dry ingredients and stir until blended. Do not overmix—a few lumps are okay.

3 Fold in the sprinkles. Be careful not to overmix, or the color will bleed into the batter. Pour the batter into the prepared pan and bake until golden around the edges and a toothpick poked into the center comes out clean, about 30 minutes. Let cool completely in the pan on a wire rack, then use the parchment paper to lift the cake from the pan. Slice into 25 squares.

4 Divide the cake bites into groups of five. Working with one cake square at a time, cover the top with frosting, then press on pearls, sprinkles, or candies in a single color. Use a new color for every five cakes.

Crispy ICE CREAM SANDWICHES

PREP
5 min

COOK
6 hr 30 min
(*includes freezing time*)

MAKES
12

INSPIRED by Mexican churros, these frozen bites combine CINNAMON-SPICED crispy rice treats with chocolate ice cream. They're not exactly traditional, but they're 100 percent ADDICTIVE.

INGREDIENTS

4 tablespoons unsalted butter

3½ cups mini marshmallows

¾ teaspoon ground cinnamon

5 cups crispy rice cereal

1 quart chocolate ice cream, softened

DIRECTIONS

1 Line two 8-inch square pans with parchment paper, allowing a few inches of paper to hang over the sides. In a large saucepan over medium-low heat, melt the butter. Add the marshmallows and cinnamon and cook, stirring constantly, until fully melted, about 4 minutes. Fold in the cereal until fully coated.

2 Place half the mixture in each prepared pan and press into an even layer. Place in the freezer 15 minutes to chill completely.

3 Add the ice cream to one of the pans and spread in an even layer over the rice treat. Use the parchment to lift the remaining treat from its pan, then remove the paper and press it onto the ice cream. Cover the pan with plastic and freeze until solid, about 6 hours. When ready to serve, remove the treats from the pan and cut into squares. Serve immediately.

Piglet Cupcakes
(page 274)

Prince Naveen
Cupcakes
(page 274)

Abu Cupcakes
(page 275)

Character CAKES

Pick a treat from this SWEET collection as the starting point for a PARTY theme or as a FANCIFUL addition to an everyday gathering. Go ahead and save time by using boxed mix for the cupcakes. Your guests will be so IMPRESSED with your DECORATING SKILLS, they'll never notice it's not homemade!

Donald Duck-Cakes (page 276)

Cheshire Cat Cupcakes (page 276)

Flower Cupcakes (page 277)

Panda Cupcakes (page 277)

PIGLET CUPCAKES

PREP: 25 min • COOK: 35 min • MAKES: 12 cupcakes

INGREDIENTS

12 unfrosted vanilla cupcakes

1½ cups white frosting

Red food coloring

1 small tube black decorating gel

12 small candy hearts

24 red fish-shaped candies

24 toothpicks

DIRECTIONS

1 Use a knife to trim the sides of each cupcake above the baking paper to shape Piglet's face (the tapered portion will be the top of his head). Place a few tablespoons of the black decorating gel in a bowl, and tint the frosting pink with the red food coloring.

2 Trim the tails from the fish candies. Halve 12 toothpicks, then slide a fish onto each as if making a lollipop.

3 Working with one cupcake at a time, cover its top with pink frosting. Add a candy heart nose to the center, as shown. Use a toothpick to apply black gel eyes, brows, and a mouth. Use the toothpick end of two fish candies to attach them on the top of the head for the ears. Repeat with the remaining cupcakes and ingredients.

PRINCE NAVEEN CUPCAKES

PREP: 25 min • COOK: 35 min • MAKES: 12 cupcakes

INGREDIENTS

1½ cups white frosting

Green food coloring

12 large green gumdrops

12 mini marshmallows

12 yellow fruit chew candies

12 unfrosted chocolate cupcakes

12 green jelly fruit slices

24 chocolate chips

12 toothpicks

DIRECTIONS

1 Tint the frosting with the green food coloring. Halve each gumdrop and mini marshmallow. Use a sharp knife to trim each fruit chew candy into a crown, as shown

2 Working with one cupcake at a time, cover the center of a cupcake with frosting, leaving a ½-inch border. Press on a fruit slice mouth and a gumdrop half for each eyelid, as shown. Attach two chocolate chips to the sticky side of two marshmallow halves, then press into place on the eyelids. Use a toothpick to add a fruit chew crown. Repeat with the remaining cupcakes and ingredients.

FRUIT CHEW CANDY CROWN HOW-TO ➴

ABU CUPCAKES

PREP: 5 min • COOK: 40 min • MAKES: 12 cupcakes

INGREDIENTS

24 caramel candies

12 large green gumdrops

⅓ cup white frosting

Red food coloring

12 unfrosted chocolate cupcakes

1½ cups chocolate frosting

24 mini chocolate chips

24 sliced almonds

DIRECTIONS

1 Roll out half the caramel candies. Use a mini heart cutter to shape them. Repeat with the remaining caramels, shaping each with a mini oval cutter. Use a toothpick to poke nostrils into each oval, as shown. Set aside. Trim the flat end from each gumdrop for the hat brims. Use the remaining dome-shaped pieces to trim small hat shapes for each brim. Attach them to the brims with their sticky ends. Set aside. Tint half the white frosting with the red food coloring. Place it and the remaining white frosting in piping bags fit with small writing tips.

2 Working with one cupcake at a time, cover the top with chocolate frosting. Layer on a caramel heart and oval for the face, as shown. Pipe on two white frosting eyes and press a mini chocolate chip pupil into each. Add a mouth with the red frosting. Press on two almond ears and a gumdrop hat, as shown. If needed, the hat can be attached with a toothpick. Repeat with the remaining cupcakes and decorating ingredients.

DONALD DUCK-CAKES

PREP: 25 min • COOK: 30 min • MAKES: 12 cupcakes

INGREDIENTS

12 yellow jelly fruit slices

12 unfrosted vanilla cupcakes

1½ cups white frosting

24 small black jelly beans

1 small tube black decorating gel

DIRECTIONS

1 Use a knife to make a deep score line in each fruit slice.

2 Working with one cupcake at a time, cover with white frosting, then use a knife to pull the frosting up into a few feathery peaks along the top, as shown. Add a fruit slice bill and two jelly bean eyes. Pipe on two black decorating gel brows. Repeat with the remaining cupcakes and ingredients.

CHESHIRE CAT CUPCAKES

PREP 5 min • COOK: 35 min • MAKES: 12 cupcakes

INGREDIENTS

24 yellow chocolate gem candies

Black food writer

6 mini white fruit chew strips

12 large purple gumdrops

Magenta or bright pink food coloring

1 cup white frosting

12 unfrosted purple cupcakes*

12 purple licorice pastels

DIRECTIONS

1 Draw a pupil onto each chocolate gem with the food writer. Halve the fruit chews, then trim a smile from each, as shown. Use a toothpick to press indents into each smile to form teeth. Trim each gumdrop into a pair of ears and use the food coloring to tint the frosting magenta. Place the frosting in a piping bag fit with a small writing tip.

2 Working with one cupcake at a time, cover one half of the cupcake with frosting to form the base of the mouth, as shown. Press on a fruit chew smile and licorice nose. Use more frosting to attach a pair of eyes. Pipe a tuft of hair at the top of the cupcake, as shown, and add a pair of gumdrop ears. If necessary, the ears can be attached with toothpicks. Repeat with the remaining cupcakes and decorating ingredients.

*To make purple cupcakes, use purple or a combination of red and blue food coloring to tint white or vanilla cake batter and bake as usual.

FLOWER CUPCAKES

PREP: 25 min • COOK: 45 min • MAKES: 12 cupcakes

INGREDIENTS

12 unfrosted chocolate cupcakes

6 white fruit chew candies

2 pink fruit chew candies

1½ cups white frosting

1 small tube blue sparkle decorating gel

24 medium white sugar pearls

36 brown chocolate gem candies

DIRECTIONS

1 Place the frosting in a piping bag fit with a medium round tip. Roll out the white and pink fruit chew candies. With a mini oval cutter, cut 3 shapes from each white candy, then halve each of the ovals. Cut the pink candies into 12 thin, ½-inch-long strips.

2 Working with one cupcake at a time, pipe a line of white icing down the center of the cupcake. Add a V-shaped tuft of frosting hair at the top. Use a dot of frosting to attach an oval half to each side of the frosting stripe for the mask, and a third half at the bottom for the muzzle.

3 Squeeze on dots of blue decorating gel for eyes and add a white sugar pearl to each. Shape a strip of the pink fruit chew candy into a smile and attach with a tiny dot of frosting applied with a toothpick. Press on a chocolate gem nose and ears, as shown. Repeat steps 2 and 3 with the remaining cupcakes and ingredients.

PANDA CUPCAKES

PREP: 5 min • COOK: 30 min • MAKES: 12 cupcakes

INGREDIENTS

24 large black gumdrops

1½ cups white frosting

Black food coloring

12 unfrosted chocolate cupcakes

24 mini chocolate chips

DIRECTIONS

1 Roll a gumdrop flat and use a mini oval cutter to shape two ovals from the candy. Repeat with the remaining candy, cutting a total of 24 ovals (we used a slightly smaller cutter to shape the ears). Use the scraps to trim 12 noses. Tint ¼ cup of the frosting with the black food coloring. Place it in a piping bag fit with a small writing tip. Place ¼ of the white frosting in a piping bag.

2 Working with one cupcake at a time, cover the cupcake with white frosting. Press on two gumdrop eyes and a pair of ears. Use the bagged white frosting to pipe on two eyes and press a mini chocolate chip pupil in the center of each. Finish by adding a gumdrop nose and piping on a black frosting mouth. Then repeat with the remaining cupcakes and decorating ingredients.

Deep Sea JELLYFISH CAKE

PREP
5 min

COOK
1 hr 45 min
(*includes chilling time*)

SERVES
About 10

WIN over fans of Nemo, Ariel, Moana, or any ocean-centered FAIRY TALE with an aquatic cake. Once it's frosted, you can DIVE right into no-stress decorating—all you need are snack cakes, a handful of candies, and a spoonful of your FAVORITE sprinkles.

INGREDIENTS

Cooking spray

1 (15-ounce) box vanilla cake mix

3 cups white frosting

Blue food coloring

2 pink coconut snack cakes

Red sour fruit strips

Fish candies

Fish sprinkles

White nonpareils

⅓ cup vanilla wafer cookie crumbs

Seashell sprinkles

Chocolate candy rocks

DIRECTIONS

1 Coat two 8- or 9-inch round cake pans with cooking spray. Prepare the cake mix according to the package directions and evenly divide the batter between the two pans. Bake as directed. Let cool in the pans 10 minutes, then turn out onto a rack to cool completely.

2 Tint the frosting with blue food coloring and place in a piping bag fit with a large writing tip. (If you're not able to fit all the frosting in your piping bag, keep the extra covered with plastic.)

3 Set one cake on a baking sheet and pipe a layer of frosting on the top. Spread evenly, then top with the other cake. Pipe and spread a thin layer of frosting all over the cake and refrigerate 30 minutes. While the cake chills, halve a few of the sour fruit strips lengthwise.

4 Transfer the cake to your serving platter. Cover evenly with the remaining frosting. Press the snack cakes in place on top and add fruit strip tentacles, as shown. Embellish the sides of the cake with the candy and sprinkle fish, and add nonpareils to the sides and top of the cake.

5 Scatter the cookie crumbs around the perimeter of the cake and add seashell sprinkles and chocolate candy rocks, as shown.

U_p-CAKES

PREP
25 min

COOK
35 min

MAKES
12 cupcakes

Capture the **ICONIC SCENE** from *Up* in cupcake form, then watch the candy-topped desserts **FLY** right off the table.

INGREDIENTS

1½ cups white frosting

12 yellow square fruit chew candies

Blue food coloring

12 unfrosted cupcakes

72 gumballs of various colors

12 pretzel sticks

DIRECTIONS

1 Place ¼ cup of the frosting in a piping bag fit with a small writing tip. Tint the remaining frosting with blue food coloring. Slightly flatten each of the fruit chew candies, then trim into a house shape. Break the pretzel sticks to form the roof pieces, as shown. Discard the remaining pieces.

2 Working with one cupcake at a time, cover with blue frosting. Press several gumballs onto one end of the cupcake, as shown. Attach a fruit chew house and pretzel roof on the opposite end, then pipe on balloon strings. Repeat with the remaining cupcakes and ingredients.

Helpful **TIP**

For a perfectly shaped layer of the blue base frosting, use a piping bag fit with a large, round tip to apply it. Hold the bag in the center of the cake and push the frosting out of the bag so that it forms a round dollop. Spread the frosting to the edges of the cupcake with a small offset spatula.

BIRTHDAYS and SWEET OCCASIONS : 281

Will-o'-the-Wisp MERINGUES

PREP
5 min

COOK
4 hr
(includes baking and drying time)

MAKES
3 dozen meringues

If you've never made meringues, you'll be **PLEASANTLY** surprised to discover how simple they are to bake. We like the mix-and-match look of **PIPING** both dollops and swirls with a star tip, but using a plain tip will produce a similarly **MAGICAL** look.

INGREDIENTS

4 egg whites, at room temperature

½ teaspoon cream of tartar

1 cup caster sugar

¼ teaspoon peppermint extract

Blue food coloring

DIRECTIONS

1. Heat oven to 200°F. Line two baking sheets with parchment paper.

2. In a stand mixer fit with a whisk attachment and set at medium speed, beat the egg whites until foamy. Add the cream of tartar and 1 tablespoon sugar. Continue to beat, adding the remaining sugar 1 tablespoon at a time, until stiff peaks form, about 6 minutes. Add the peppermint extract, tint with blue food coloring, and beat until well blended.

3. Place the meringue in a piping bag fit with a large star tip. Pipe 2- to 3-inch dollops and swirls on each prepared baking sheet, spacing them 1 inch apart. Bake 2 hours. Do not open the oven door. Turn off the heat and leave the meringues inside the oven to continue to dry out for at least 2 hours. Store in an airtight container until ready to serve.

Woody Sheriff Badge COOKIES

PREP
10 min

COOK
50 min

MAKES
About 2 dozen cookies

Bake of **BATCH** of these double-decker cookies for your posse in lieu of a cake. They make a **GREAT** addition to a cowboy-themed birthday or any **CELEBRATION** spread.

INGREDIENTS

1 batch sugar cookie dough (see Conversation Mouse Cookies, page 198)

1 cup white frosting

Yellow food coloring

Gold sanding sugar

1 cup yellow chocolate gem candies

DIRECTIONS

1. Heat the oven to 350°F and line two baking sheets with parchment paper. Set aside one-third of the dough. Gather the remaining two-thirds and roll it out to ¼-inch thickness. Use a large star cutter to shape the dough into stars. Arrange them on the baking sheets, spacing them 2 inches apart. Gather and reroll the dough as needed.

2. Roll out the remaining portion of dough as described in Step 1. Use a small star cutter to shape a star for each larger star cookie. Transfer the stars to a baking sheet and arrange in the remaining space on the pans. Gather and reroll the dough as needed.

3. Bake the cookies until set and slightly crisp, turning them once halfway through, about 12 minutes. Let the cookies cool on the pans for 5 minutes, then transfer them to a rack to cool completely.

4. Tint the frosting with the yellow food coloring and place it in a piping bag fit with a small writing tip. Place the sanding sugar in a small bowl. Working with one small star cookie a time, pipe on and spread it with frosting, then sprinkle with sanding sugar, letting the excess fall back into the bowl. Set aside and repeat with the remaining frosting and small stars. Attach each frosted star to a larger star with frosting, as shown. Finish by attaching chocolate gems to the tips of each cookie with more frosting.

Cruella COOKIES

PREP
10 min

COOK
1 hr 30 min
*(includes
cooling and
setting time)*

MAKES
About 3 dozen

The **SLEEK**, two-toned embellishment on these sugar cookies comes from **DIPPING** them in white and dark chocolate—a **DECADENT** tribute to a very fashionable villain.

INGREDIENTS

1 batch sugar cookie dough (see Conversation Mouse Cookies, page 198)

1 cup white chocolate chips

1 cup high-quality dark chocolate chips

Jumbo heart sprinkles

DIRECTIONS

1 Heat the oven to 350°F and line two baking sheets with parchment paper. Roll out the dough to ¼-inch thickness. Use a 2½- to 3-inch round cutter to shape the dough into circles. Arrange them on the baking sheets, spacing them 2 inches apart. Gather and reroll the dough as needed.

2 Bake the cookies until set and slightly crisp, turning them once halfway through, about 12 minutes. Let the cookies cool on the pans for 5 minutes, then transfer them to a rack to cool completely. Cover the baking sheets with fresh paper and set aside.

3 Melt the white chocolate chips in a heat-safe bowl according to the package directions. Dip the edge of each cookie into the chocolate, as shown, letting the excess fall back into the bowl. If needed, use the flat edge of a butter knife to scrape away any extra chocolate from the back of the cookies. Place the cookies on a prepared baking sheet and let the chocolate set. Repeat the steps with the dark chocolate, dipping the opposite side. Attach a heart sprinkle mouth to each cookie with a bit of melted chocolate applied with a toothpick. Let set completely before serving.

Tigger PUMPKIN CUPS

PREP
5 min

COOK
2 hr 30 min
(*includes chilling time*)

MAKES
2 dozen

TOPPED with chocolate stripes and filled with warm **SPICES**, there's only one stuffy from the Hundred Acre Wood that could **INSPIRE** these two-bite **TREATS**.

INGREDIENTS

1¾ cups sugar

¾ cup condensed milk

1 teaspoon vanilla extract

Pinch of kosher salt

½ teaspoon pumpkin pie spice

6 tablespoons pumpkin puree

12 ounces white chocolate chips

1 cup mini marshmallows

⅓ cup high-quality dark chocolate chips

DIRECTIONS

1 Line a mini muffin tin with 24 paper liners. In a medium saucepan over medium-high heat, combine the sugar, milk, vanilla, salt, and pumpkin pie spice and bring to a boil. Let boil 4 minutes, whisking constantly. Remove from the heat and whisk in the pumpkin puree, white chocolate chips, and marshmallows until melted. Transfer to a liquid measuring cup or small bowl with a spout.

2 Fill the prepared muffin wells with the mixture. Refrigerate until set, about 2 hours.

3 Melt the dark chocolate chips in a small, heat-safe bowl according to the package directions. Use a toothpick to draw stripes on each pumpkin cup, as shown. Return the cups to the refrigerator and chill until the chocolate is set, about 10 minutes. Keep refrigerated until ready to serve.

Pocahontas FEATHER POPS

PREP
5 min

COOK
15 min

MAKES
6 pops

Fashioned after Pocahontas's **FEATHERED EARRINGS**, these crisp lollipops are made with **PIECRUST**. We kept the icing white, but you can add a few drops of **EDIBLE COLOR** if you like.

INGREDIENTS

1 egg

Flour, for dusting

1 refrigerated piecrust

1 cup confectioners' sugar

2 tablespoons coconut milk

¼ teaspoon vanilla extract

Special equipment

6 (6-inch) lollipop sticks

4- to 5-inch feather cookie cutter

DIRECTIONS

1 Heat the oven to 400°F. Line a baking sheet with parchment paper.

2 Whisk the egg with 1 tablespoon water. On a lightly floured surface, roll out the piecrust dough to a ¼-inch thickness. Use the feather cookie cutter to cut the dough into 12 feathers. Use a spatula to transfer half the feathers to the prepared baking sheet. Brush each with the egg wash and press a lollipop stick in the center. Sandwich each with a plain feather by gently pressing it on top.

3 Bake the pops until golden around the edges, about 10 minutes. Use a spatula to transfer the pops to a wire rack to cool completely.

4 Sift the confectioners' sugar into a small bowl. Stir in the coconut milk 2 teaspoons at a time until you have a smooth, spreadable icing. Frost each pop, then let the icing set. Use a toothpick to etch a line down the center of each feather.

Buzz Lightyear Galaxy CAKE POPS

PREP
18 min

COOK
50 min

MAKES
About 18

SPARKLY sanding sugar, starry sprinkles, and an uncomplicated dipping technique give these pops their OUT-OF-THIS-WORLD appearance. Don't be discouraged if the first one or two only have a few SWIRLS; the patterns will become more DRAMATIC as you dip.

INGREDIENTS

8 cups cake crumbs

½ cup plus 2 tablespoons vanilla frosting

Silver sanding sugar

Silver star sprinkles

½ cup white candy melts

Vegetable oil

½ cup dark blue candy melts

¼ cup turquoise candy melts

¼ cup purple candy melts

Special equipment

18 lollipop sticks

Foam block

DIRECTIONS

1 Line a baking sheet with parchment paper. In a large bowl, stir together the cake crumbs and frosting until well blended. Roll the mixture into heaping tablespoon-size balls and freeze until firm but not frozen, about 10 minutes. Transfer to the refrigerator.

2 Place the sprinkles in small bowls and ready a foam block for holding the finished pops. In a heat-safe bowl, melt the white candy melts according to the package directions. If needed, add a few drops of vegetable oil to make the melted candy less viscous. Repeat with the dark blue, turquoise, and purple candy melts. Pour each color melt into the center of the white candy melt bowl. Use a skewer or the thin handle of a utensil to swirl the colors, stirring just a few turns (blending too much will muddle the colors).

3 Remove three pops from the refrigerator. Dip the end of a lollipop stick into the melted candy, then insert it into a pop. Repeat with the remaining two pops. Working with one pop at a time, dip it into the candy, swirl it once, then remove and tap off the excess candy. Scatter immediately with sanding sugar and star sprinkles, then use the stick of the pop to stand it in the foam block and let the candy set. Repeat with the other two pops.

4 Continue the dipping steps with the remaining pops, removing just a few from the refrigerator at a time so they remain cooled before dipping. Keep cool until ready to serve.

Hidden Mickey BLUEBERRY SLAB PIE

PREP
5 min

COOK
1 hr (includes cooling time)

SERVES
About 15

If you're not **FAMILIAR** with this casual sheet pan dessert, allow us to introduce you: it has all the **TASTY** qualities of a pie baked in a plate but the benefit of more servings and less mess. (Yes please!) We chose **THE MOUSE** as a subtle decoration for the top, but you could use the same technique for another **FAVORITE** character shape—just keep it simple!

INGREDIENTS

4 cups fresh blueberries

½ cup sugar

½ teaspoon orange zest plus juice of 1 orange

½ teaspoon cinnamon

⅛ teaspoon ground ginger

Pinch kosher salt

1 tablespoon cornstarch mixed with 2 tablespoons water

3 refrigerated piecrusts (from two 15-ounce packages)

Flour, for dusting

1 egg

Coarse sugar

Special equipment
Mini Mickey Mouse cookie cutter

DIRECTIONS

1 In a medium saucepan over medium-low heat, combine 3 cups blueberries with the sugar, orange zest and juice, cinnamon, ginger, and salt. Bring to a simmer, then continue to cook until the berries begin to burst, about 5 minutes. Add the cornstarch mixture and simmer, stirring frequently, until thickened, about 2 minutes. Remove from the heat and stir in the remaining berries. Let cool 10 minutes.

2 Meanwhile, heat the oven to 375°F. Gather all the dough into a ball and halve. Flatten each portion into a rectangular disk. Set one aside. On a lightly floured surface, roll the other portion into a 12-by-18-inch rectangle. Drape the dough over your rolling pin and unfurl into a 9-by-13-inch rimmed baking sheet, letting the excess dough hang over the edges. Press into the pan. Evenly spread the blueberry mixture in the crust.

3 On a lightly floured surface, roll out the remaining portion of dough. Use a mini Mickey Mouse cookie cutter to cut several holes into the center of the crust, as shown, reserving the cut pieces. Drape the dough over the filling. Pinch together the top and bottom crusts and trim the excess down to a 1-inch width. Tuck the excess dough under itself to form a crust, then crimp with the tines of a fork.

4 In a small bowl, whisk the egg with 1 tablespoon water. Brush the top of the pie with the egg wash, then add the Mickey dough pieces and brush once more. Sprinkle with coarse sugar. Bake until golden and the filling begins to bubble, about 30 minutes. Let cool slightly before slicing and serving.

Mini Magnolia BLOSSOM TARTS

PREP
5 min

COOK
45 min

MAKES
12

Translated into English, the Chinese name *Mulan* means MAGNOLIA. It's a fitting moniker for a young warrior girl from the countryside where the flowers BLOSSOM in spring. In this recipe, they take shape as DELICATE pastries filled with a rich dark chocolate ganache.

INGREDIENTS

Flour, for dusting

1 (15-ounce) package refrigerated pie dough

4 ounces high-quality dark chocolate chips

⅓ cup heavy cream

2 teaspoons unsalted butter

¼ teaspoon vanilla extract

Pinch kosher salt

⅓ cup pink candy melts

Pink nonpareils

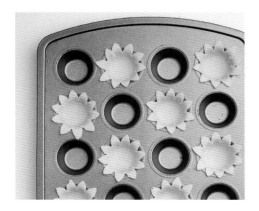

DIRECTIONS

1 Heat the oven to 450°F. On a lightly floured surface, roll a dough portion out to ¼-inch thickness. Use a 3½- to 4-inch flower cutter to shape it into 6 flowers. Press each into a mini pie pan, staggering them so the pieces don't touch. Repeat with the remaining portion of dough. Bake until set and beginning to brown slightly, about 5 minutes. Let cool in the pan.

2 Combine the chocolate chips, heavy cream, and butter in a heat-safe bowl. Place an inch of water in a saucepan and set over medium heat, then fit the bowl with the chocolate on top. It should not touch the water. Bring the water to a simmer and warm the mixture, whisking frequently, until the chocolate is melted, fully blended, and smooth. Add the vanilla and salt, and whisk to combine.

3 Spoon the ganache into each flower cup, filling it to just below the rim. Gently tap the pan on your work surface so that the ganache has a smooth top, then transfer the tarts to the refrigerator and chill until firm, about 3 hours.

4 Place the candy melts in a heat-safe bowl and melt according to the package directions. Working with one tart at a time, spoon a dollop of the melted candy onto the tart, then sprinkle lightly with nonpareils. Repeat with the remaining tarts, candy, and sprinkles. Return the tarts to the refrigerator and chill until the candy is set, about 10 minutes. Keep chilled until ready to serve.

Liar's DESSERT DICE

PREP
5 min

COOK
2 hr 45 min
(includes
chilling time)

MAKES
About 18

A game of liar's dice doomed **BOOTSTRAP BILL TURNER** to an eternity aboard the *Flying Dutchman*. This edible version, made with white fudge and mini chocolate chips, is a much surer bet—**IN YOUR FAVOR**.

INGREDIENTS

1½ cups granulated sugar

⅔ cup evaporated milk

2 tablespoons butter

1 cup mini marshmallows

2 cups white chocolate chips

2 teaspoons vanilla extract

¾ cup mini chocolate chips

DIRECTIONS

1 Line a loaf pan with parchment paper, letting it hang over the edges slightly. In a large saucepan over medium heat, whisk together the sugar, evaporated milk, and butter. Bring to a boil, whisking constantly. Boil for 5 minutes, continuing to whisk. Remove the pan from the heat.

2 Add the marshmallows, white chocolate chips, and vanilla extract to the pan, and whisk vigorously until smooth. Pour the fudge into the prepared pan and chill until firm but not hard, about 2 hours.

3 Use the parchment paper to lift the fudge from the pan. Slice into 1¼-inch cubes. Use a toothpick to make divots in each cube where the dots will go (use real dice as a guide). Insert a chocolate chip, flat side up, into each divot. Refrigerate until ready to serve.

Mickey and Minnie CUPCAKES

PREP
5 min

COOK
50 min

MAKES
12

This duo of **CHOCOLATE-STUDDED CUPCAKES** offers a chearful finale to any party.

INGREDIENTS

3 cups white frosting

12 unfrosted chocolate cupcakes

Silver sanding sugar

Gold sanding sugar (optional)

12 mini chocolate-covered cookies

24 brown chocolate gem candies

Pink food coloring

Red food coloring

Black food coloring

Yellow food coloring

12 jumbo heart sprinkles

DIRECTIONS

1 Use 1 cup of the frosting to cover the tops of all the cupcakes. Sprinkle the center of 6 cupcakes with the silver sanding sugar, and if using, the remaining cupcakes with gold. Press a chocolate cookie face and pair of chocolate gem ears onto the center of each cupcake.

2 Evenly divide the remaining frosting among 6 bowls. Use the pink food coloring to tint three bowls in varying shades of pink. Use the red, black, and yellow food coloring to tint the remaining bowls (one with each color). Place each color of tinted frosting in a piping bag fit with a small star tip. Use the pink frosting to decorate the silver sprinkled cupcakes, and the red, yellow, and black frosting to decorate the remaining cupcakes, as shown. For the pink Minnie cupcakes, pipe a generous dot of pink frosting between each pair of mouse ears and add two heart sprinkles to form a bow.

Serpent's
Stew
(page 145)

Frozen Snowflakes
(page 227)

Disney EATS

Fill your table with an entire spread of INSPIRED DISHES!
With the help of a few DISNEY FRIENDS, these menu ideas
will help you summon delight (and DELICIOUSNESS!)
at your NEXT meal, whether it's an everyday dinner
or a more SPECIAL occasion. We've even included
a few special themes to spark your IMAGINATION.

3 COZY MEALS for OMNIVORES

LADY AND THE TRAMP SHEET PAN MEATBALLS and
GRAVY (page 154) + ALADDIN'S FATTOUSH SALAD (page 94)

JESSIE'S COWGIRL SALAD with CORN BREAD
CROUTONS (page 105) + WOODY'S COWBOY CHILI (page 127)

SAUSAGE KALE PIZZA (page 181) +
CRYSTAL PALACE PASTA SALAD (page 97)

3 COZY MEALS for VEGETARIANS

MAGIC CARPET FLATBREAD (page 122) +
ALADDIN'S FATTOUSH SALAD (page 94)

MULAN'S BLOSSOM STIR-FRY (page 141) +
LUNAR NEW YEAR VEGGIE DUMPLINGS (page 197)

REMY'S RATATOUILLE with POACHED EGGS (page 169)
+ KRONK'S SPINACH PUFFS (page 165)

COOKIES + COCOA

BAYMAX COCOA (page 62)

CRUELLA COOKIES (page 286)

WILL-O'-THE-WISP MERINGUES (page 282)

CAPTAIN HOOK BROWNIE BITES (page 235)

FEAST FOR A PRINCESS

BELLE'S BOOZE-LESS FRENCH 75 (page 52)

MINI CHEESE BALL MICE (page 70)

MRS. POTTS MELON SALAD (page 98)

ROYAL ROAST CHICKEN (page 188)

MINI MAGNOLIA BLOSSOM TARTS (page 297)

WILD PARTY BITES

SPIRIT-FREE SERENGETI SPRITZ (page 52)

KING OF ALL VEGGIE PLATTERS (page 46)

PANDA CUPCAKES (page 277)

TIGGER PUMPKIN CUPS (page 289)

GAME NIGHT NIBBLES

NIGHT HOWLER LEMONADE (page 73)

LADY AND THE TRAMP PUPPY MIX (page 49)

STOPLIGHT CAPRESE SKEWERS (page 78)

TIANA'S SHRIMP and REMOULADE (page 114)

LIAR'S DESSERT DICE (page 298)

SUMMER SPREAD

YETI'S YELLOW LEMON SLUSH (page 53)

NEVER GROWING UP
TUNA SAILBOATS (page 101)

LUIGI'S HOT DOG DIPPERS (page 110)

LILO'S TROPICAL FRUIT CONES
with KAHLÚA DRIZZLE (page 66)

SAND DOLLAR COOKIES (page 244)

WHIMSICAL BRUNCH

PLAYFUL PICNIC

ACKNOWLEDGMENTS

There are so many who have helped bring this project to life, and have also helped me become the cook and writer that I am today. I likely won't remember everyone, but this is my best attempt. First and foremost, to Pat Van Note, who took a giant leap of faith when she handed me not one, but two book-length projects. Your generosity is greatly appreciated, and your seasoned advice, candid humor, and unwavering support were THE guiding force for this book. Thank you.

Much gratitude also goes to the rest of the Disney team with whom I collaborated—Jennifer Levesque, Monica Vasquez, Alan Kaplan, Scott Piehl, Jennifer Black, Megan Speer, Warren Meislin, Dania Kurtz, Marybeth Tregarthen, Karen Romano, Kate Milford, and the rest of the production crew, and most especially David Roe, who graciously made 900 bajillion edits and let me break the rules by meddling with his wonderful page layouts. A big thank you also to Laura Palese for the original book design and Suzanne Fass for her expert indexing skills.

I can't take full credit for all the ideas found in these pages. Recipes shared by the Disney Family editors, the chefs at Be Our Guest, The Crystal Palace, Disney's Polynesian Village Resort, Meredith Bond Steele, Shelby Chambers, Tiffany Davis, Rosie DeLibero, Li Ming Lee, Vickie Liu; Jessica McDonald; Kate O'Leary; Irene Lee; Jen Wood; and Elise Apffel, are also here. Thank you for your contributions. This book wouldn't be complete without them. Enormous gratitude also goes to the creators behind all the Disney franchises represented. The worlds and characters you have created are truly inspiring. I am grateful to have had the opportunity to be a part.

To the photo crew: Joanna Chattman your eye for light made every recipe come to life. Ann Lewis, thank you for being both the ears and the eyes of the project both on set and off. Laura Manning, I could not have done the styling of this book without you beside me. Thanks for your obsessive attention to detail, and for keeping me laughing the entire way through. Many thanks also go to assistants Georgia Teensma (music and photo editing goddess), Kaitlyn Ferrari (expert organizer), and Montgomery Sheridan (enthusiastic hand model).

For my fellow food, editorial, and creative people who have offered me advice and opportunity past and present, a big thanks to Betty Rosbottom, Molly Shuster, Jenna Helwig, Nicole Folino, Danielle Naugler, Deanna Cook, Debra Immergut, Sally Ekus, Lisa Ekus, Mary Reilly, Dominic Perri, Devon O'Brien, and Carolyn Malcoun. A thank you isn't big enough for Ryan Cline whose friendship and professional advice I treasure deeply, and who convinced me years ago that I could turn my passion into a new path. And Laurel Brandsetter, a real bestie, my biggest cheerleader, and a badass business woman who knows the right answer to literally everything.

I am forever indebted to my mother, Sandy Lowe, and aunt Lucy Dillard, from whom I inherited my love of cooking—most especially for other people. You are both a part of everything I do, large and small. Thank you also to my brother Les Howard and dad, Brian Lowe.

And most importantly, to Chris, Andiyah, Inez, and Zadie: you are the key ingredients to everything that is good. Thank you for your willingness to wash piles of dishes, eat a thousand iterations of the same meal, and for enduring the mayhem that is our kitchen. I am happiest when I sit down to dinner with all of you.

INDEX

A

Abu (*Aladdin*)
  Abu Cupcakes, 272, 275
Aladdin (*Aladdin*)
  Aladdin's Fattoush Salad, 94
Alice (*Alice in Wonderland*)
  Alice's Teensy Tea Party Lunch, 106–109
Aliens (*Toy Story*)
  Alien Toast for Two, 22
All Souped Up, 124–127
Andy (*Toy Story*)
  Pizza Planet Duo, 178–181
Animal (*The Muppets*)
  Punk Rock Pink Animal Pasta, 121
Anna (*Frozen*)
  Frozen Pops, 236
Apple Bowl, Snow White's, 29
Apple-Cinnamon Pop, Snow White's, 64
Apple Slice Sandwiches, Hidden Mickey, 61

Ariel (*The Little Mermaid*)
  Ariel's Deep Blueberry Sea Bowl, 29
  Sand Dollar Cookies, 244
Aristocat-ic Quiche Marie, 129
Arlo (*The Good Dinosaur*)
  Arlo's Kale Chips, 54
arugula pesto, 133
Aunt Cass (*Big Hero 6*)
  Aunt Cass's Wings, 184
avocado, preventing browning, 22

B

Bagel Bites, Pinocchio, 113
baking tips, 15. *See also* tools
Baklava Bites, 243
Baloo (*The Jungle Book*)
  Bare Necessities Chocolate Coins, 247
  Mowgli's Pawpaw Smoothie, 77
Balsamic Chicken Legs, Tow Mater's, 162
Bambi (*Bambi*)
  Bambi Bento, 86
Banana Dalmatian Pops, Frozen, 58
Bare Necessities Chocolate Coins, 247
Basic Gingerbread Dough, 226
Basil Syrup, 53
Baymax (*Big Hero 6*)
  Baymax Cocoa, 62

Baymax Cookies, 225, 227
Bayou Andouille and Collards, 187
bear sandwich, 89
beet sauce, 121
Belle (*Beauty and the Beast*)
  Belle's Booze-less French 75, 51, 52
  Belle's Enchanted Quinoa Porridge, 35
bento
  Bambi Bento, 86
  Brave Bear Bento, 89
  Lightning McQueen Bento, 90
  Olaf Bento, 93
  Pirate Bento, 85
Big Top Candy Cane Cupcakes, Dumbo's, 229
Birthdays and Sweet Occasions, 261–301
  menu suggestions, 304–308
Blossom Stir-Fry, Mulan's, 141
Blue Corn Tacos, Dante's, 138
Blueberry Bowl, Ariel's, 29
Blueberry Slab Pie, Hidden Mickey, 294
Bo Peep (*Toy Story*)
  Mini (No Meat!) Shepherdess Pies, 142
Bonnie (*Toy Story 3*)
  Forky Pretzels, 259
boosting nutrition, 61
Bootstrap Bill Turner (Pirates of the Caribbean)
  Liar's Dessert Dice, 298

C

Chocolate Cutout Cookies, 221
Chocolate Sandwich Cookies, Maleficent, 262
Chocolate-Topped Rice Cakes, Jack's, 222
chocolate, working with, 16
choosing potatoes, 26
chutney, green, 117
Cinderella (*Cinderella*)
  Cinderella's Dreamy Pumpkin Waffles, 36
Conch Shell Mac and Cheese, 172
Cookie Pretzel Bark, Mickey, 249, 250
cookies
  Basic Gingerbread Dough, 226
  Baymax Cookies, 225, 227
  Conversation Mouse Cookies, 198
  Cruella Cookies, 286
  Frozen Snowflakes, 224, 227
  Gingerbread Five Ways, 224–227
  M and M Milk Toppers, 239

Maleficent Triple Chocolate Sandwich Cookies, 262
menu suggestion, 305
Mexican Chocolate Cutout Cookies, 221
Mickey Cookies, 225, 227
Minnie Cookies, 225, 227
Nutcracker Cookies, 224, 226
Sand Dollar Cookies, 244
Sugar Skull Cookies, 221
White Rabbit's Petite Pocket Watch Cookies, 106, 109
Woody Sheriff Badge Cookies, 285
cooking tips, 14–16, 22, 26, 35, 46, 54, 61, 81, 97, 129, 130, 201, 281. *See also* Helpful Tools
cooking with kids, 14
corn bread croutons, 105
Cowboy Chili, Woody's, 125, 127
Cowgirl Salad, Jessie's, 105
cream cheese frosting, 215
Creature Cakes, 272–277
Crispy Ice Cream Sandwiches, 270
Crudité Two Ways, 208–211
Cruella De Vil (*101 Dalmatians*)
  Cruella Cookies, 286
Crystal Palace Pasta Salad, 97
cucumber syrup, 53
cupcakes
  Abu Cupcakes, 272, 275
  Cheshire Cat Cupcakes, 273, 276
  Creature Cakes, 272–277
  Donald Duck-Cakes, 273, 276
  Dumbo's Big Top Candy Cane Cupcakes, 229
  Fireworks over Magic Kingdom Cupcakes, 194

Flower Cupcakes, 273, 277
Kitten Bow Cupcakes, 212
Mickey and Minnie Cupcakes, 301
Panda Cupcakes, 273, 277
Piglet's Cupcakes, 272, 274
Prince Naveen Cupcakes, 272, 274
Rabbit's Carrot Patch Cupcakes, 217, 219
Up-Cakes, 281
cutting strawberries how-to, 201

D

Dalmatian Frozen Banana Pops, 58
Dante (*Coco*)
  Dante's Blue Corn Tacos, 138
decorating tips, 15, 201, 202, 281. *See also* Birthdays and Sweet Occasions; cookies; cupcakes
Deep Sea Jellyfish Cake, 278
desserts and sweets. *See also* Birthdays; cakes; candy; cookies; cupcakes; Easy Treats; Everything for the Holidays

312   INDEX

Baymax Cocoa (page 62)